IN CASE
YOU'RE
CURIOUS

IN CASE YOU'RE CURIOUS

WRITTEN BY:
**Molly Alderton, Daniela Fellman
Meghan Hilton, Julie LaBarr
Planned Parenthood of the Rocky Mountains**

ILLUSTRATED BY:
Meghan Hilton

EDITED BY:
Alison Macklin

V!Va
EDITIONS

S

Published in the United States by Viva Editions, an imprint of Start Midnight, LLC, 101 Hudson Street, Thirty-Seventh Floor, Suite 3705, Jersey City, NJ 07302.

Printed in the United States.
Cover design: Allyson Fields
Cover illustrations: Meghan Hilton
Illustrations: Meghan Hilton
Text design: Frank Wiedemann
First Edition.
10 9 8 7 6 5 4 3 2 1

Trade paper ISBN: 978-1-63228-067-1
E-book ISBN: 978-1-63228-123-4

Library of Congress Cataloging-in-Publication Data is available on file.

This book is dedicated to the next generation, the youth of today. Your generation has the power to tilt the scales and make the world a better place. A place where all sex is wanted (enthusiastically consensual), a place where people can live openly without fear of discrimination because of who they love or how they identitfy. A place where people have all the information they need to make the healthiest decision for themselves. And a place where sexuality is valued. We believe in you and we are here for you!

TABLE OF CONTENTS

PREFACE

Sex. It's everywhere. Or at least that's what people always say. And honestly, it's not totally untrue—we are surrounded by sex all day, every day. We see sexual images in commercials and sing along without much care to sexual lyrics in our favorite songs. And still, the topic of sex is often hushed, shamed, and policed in ways that other areas of healthcare are not. Sexuality is part of being human and is experienced in every stage of life, so why is it so hard to talk about?

Well, there are countless answers to that question. One major part of the problem lies in how the United States approaches sex education. Most adults think young people are learning everything they need to know about sex, relationships, and their bodies in school. And while we know parents support teaching sex ed in middle and high school, it just isn't happening.[1] Believe it or not, only 24 states and the District of Columbia make schools teach sex education, and of those, only 13 states require the information provided be medically accurate.[2] Some states even have laws that dictate whether information provided on topics like sexual orientation is presented in a negative or a positive light.[3] There is a noticeable gap between what young people should be learning and what information they are actually receiving in the classroom.

At Planned Parenthood, we have been *the* trusted provider and advocate of high-quality sexual healthcare for over 100 years, and we are the largest provider of sex education in the nation. And that means when it comes to sex ed, we've heard it all: the good, the bad, and the ugly! From comparisons of sexually active people to chewed-up gum or used tape, young people in the United States have gotten some pretty dismal messages about sex and relationships over the past several decades, the sentiment regularly being that sex is unmentionable and often shameful.

But we're here to help change that! As sex educators, it's our mission to ensure young people—and all people, really—have access to the information they need, when they need it. We came to this profession because we want all sex to be consensual and pleasurable. We want everyone to be able to make their own decisions about whom they have sex with, and when, and how! We believe all people have the right to access this information free from shame. We believe that a person's sexual identity, expression, and activity is *theirs*, and it is deeply personal and unique. Because these beliefs are so intrinsic to who we are, we, the sex educators, pride ourselves on providing open and honest information in a safe and nonjudgmental way. We also recognize that we can't be everywhere for everyone. Or can we?

As a trusted leader and innovator, Planned Parenthood of the Rocky Mountains launched its textline *In Case You're Curious*, or ICYC, in 2009 to do just that—to make ourselves available to young people everywhere. So no matter where a young person lives, they can get real, personalized, confidential answers to their questions about sex and sexuality. And all of this happens exactly where young people are—on their phones! We have real sex educators who are there to answer questions, link to healthcare information, and provide additional resources—all in 160 characters or less.

The sex educators who staff the line are from diverse backgrounds and are highly trained with over 100 years of combined experience teaching sex ed. We work with a number of Planned Parenthood affiliates and health departments across the United States, growing from just 76 incoming and outgoing texts in that first year to over 7,281 texts in 2018. Our goal in providing this service is ensuring we are accessible whenever and wherever we are needed. Staff respond to questions within 24 hours and have thousands of repeat users.

ICYC isn't a hotline—it's not intended to be used for emergency situations. But we can help you navigate tough situations. We know there are lots of other really great hotlines out there doing great work (check out the resource in the wrap-up), so our goal is to connect you to those, instead of duplicating them. However, if a texter is under 18 and tells us they are being hurt, hurting someone else, or thinking of hurting themselves, we will report our conversation to police in order to help keep them safe. ICYC is a place where you can be sure you are getting current, nonjudgmental information right on your phone. The service is free (standard text messaging rates apply) and, while marketed specifically for teens, anyone can use it.

So why a book, you might ask? Well, because in the last six years we've been running ICYC, we have had over 47,000 new texts, and over 79,000 different interactions/conversations. In those numbers we have seen a lot of people have really similar questions, and we wanted to show folks that having questions is okay. Everyone (no, really—everyone) has questions about sex and sexuality. That is completely normal. We wanted to show you that you shouldn't be embarrassed to ask us. That probably, what you are asking about has been asked many times already. That even if you might think it's a totally bizarre question, we've probably heard it.

INTRODUCTION

Who's this book for? Have you ever had questions about sex? Is the book currently in your hands? Then the answer is *you*!

Welcome to *In Case You're Curious*! Teens (and, let's face it, pretty much *all people*) have so many questions about their changing bodies, what's normal, how sex works, and how to have healthy relationships. Have you always wanted to know why broken hearts hurt so bad? Has someone once told you that you can't get pregnant from precum? Well, you've come to the right place (or book)! That's why we're here. We have these answers and some you never knew you always wanted to know. Planned Parenthood's ICYC (In Case You're Curious) offers teens a confidential text-line where trained sex educators answer questions and connect teens to accurate sexual health information. ICYC has been operating since 2009, and we've heard a *lot* of questions over the years. And, interestingly, many folks out there ask questions about the same stuff. So, we decided to put this book together.

This book represents some of the most commonly asked questions we get. But, lucky for you, here we aren't limited to 160 characters in our answers! The information we are providing is basic and a quick reference. It isn't meant to replace having conversations with your family or doing further research. It is meant to help answer some of those private questions that maybe you don't want to ask your parent, teacher, or friends. Maybe you do want to ask those people, but you aren't sure how to get the conversation started. This book can help with that, too! We've also included some not-so-common questions to show you that no question is off-limits. All questions about sexual health are welcome at ICYC!

WHY SHOULDN'T I JUST SEARCH THE INTERNET FOR THESE ANSWERS?

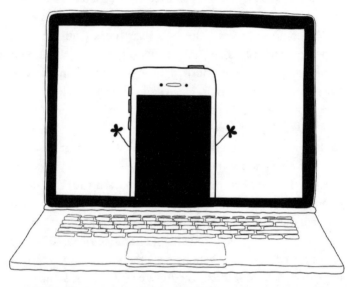

While the Internet does provide lots of answers to these questions and more, it can often take a lot of digging around, and you can't always be sure that the information you're getting is reliable or true. All the questions in this book have been answered by trained Planned Parenthood sex educators with up-to-date information (as of time of publishing). We strive to make our answers inclusive and free of stigma. It is a goal of *ICYC* to be a resource that supports people in making decisions about their sexual health. We believe trusting people with accurate information can empower them to make the best decisions throughout their lifetime.

So, AFTER READING THIS BOOK WILL I

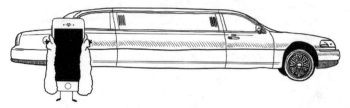

BE AN EXPERT?

ICYC answers are a great starting point. However, it would be impossible to cover all there is to know about sex and sexual health in one book. So, as you read, know that some of these answers are just the beginning.

More importantly, sex is different for everyone. Your definition of "expert" might be wildly different than someone else's definition of "expert." Sex is a subject people have a lot of different values, opinions, and thoughts on. This book is meant to be informative, but should never take the place of you figuring out what is or isn't right for you. So, take care of yourself while you're reading; maybe read while you're in a bubble bath, with friends, or while listening to your favorite playlist. We know not everyone has had control around their sexual experiences, and we want to be sensitive to this. In our Wrap Up section, we provide resources for supporting you with what you're going through. Whether it's connections to mental health services or quizzes to help you decide which birth control is best for you, *ICYC* is here for you.

WHOM SHOULD I TALK TO ABOUT THIS STUFF?

Great question! Throughout this book you will see mention of "trusted adults." Trusted adults can be any adults in your life you feel safe and comfortable having these conversations with. Some examples of trusted adults could be:

▸ Parents/guardians/caregivers/other family members

▸ Teachers

▸ Coaches

▸ Doctors/clinicians

▸ Youth group leaders

▸ Family friends

▸ And so many others

ICYC also encourages talking with partners and friends, but sometimes having a grownup with advice can be helpful in navigating the confusing world of growing up.

OKAY, ANYTHING ELSE I NEED TO KNOW BEFORE READING?

A couple housekeeping items. The first is to address some of the language we use in this book. Our questions were kept the way we received them. You might notice slang terminology, misspelled words, or incorrect grammar. We work with young people, young people ask us questions—it makes sense that their voices be present in the book.

We use the terms "person with a penis" and "person with a vagina" in our answers instead of male, female, guy, girl, etc. We use this language because not every person who has a penis identifies as male, and not every person with a vagina identifies as female (you will learn more about this in Chapter 6). At ICYC we care a lot about people getting the best information for their bodies, and so we talk very directly about those body parts and what they need to be safe and healthy. As you're reading through the book, there may be terms or words you haven't heard of before. Any word you come across that is bolded can be found with its definition in the glossary at the back of the book.

We also want people to know that their bodies can look many different ways, so—spoiler alert—there are lots of drawings of vulvas, vaginas, penises… Oh my!

All right, now that we've got the who, the what, and the why out of the way, you can go on and enjoy the book. At ICYC we take sex education very seriously, but it's our hope that you find some fun, comfort, and information in the pages of this book. And if you don't find your question or you come up with new questions, we are always happy to answer when you text "ICYC?" to 57890.

CHAPTER ONE

"CAN YOU DIE FROM MASTURBATING TOO MUCH?"

AND OTHER QUESTIONS ABOUT SEX

WHEN WILL I BE READY [TO HAVE SEX]?

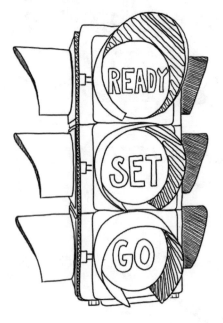

Deciding if and when to have **sex** can be a big decision that's very personal. Connecting with someone romantically, emotionally, and/or physically can be really amazing. There isn't a perfect checklist to make sure a person's ready for **sex**, but here are some things to consider that might help you decide. Do you feel comfortable talking with your partner about your boundaries, including what you want and don't want to do sexually? Have you thought about what type of protection to use and made sure you know how to use it properly? What would you do if a **pregnancy** happened or an **STI** was passed? Do you trust your partner to respect your needs? Do you feel confident in your decision? Think about it, make sure you feel comfortable, and don't ever feel like you have to do anything you're not ready for.

WHY DO PEOPLE *want* TO HAVE SEX?

People have **sex** for many reasons! Some people have **sex** because it feels good physically. Others might have **sex** to feel closer to their partner emotionally, to have a baby, to relax, to release stress, or to even exercise. Whatever the reason, it's important that it's their choice. For some people, **sex** is a really big deal, and for other people, it just isn't. You get to decide how important it is in your life.

How does sex feel?

How **sex** feels is different for everyone. Some people think **sex** is amazing, and some people have no interest in **sex** or don't like it. The reason it can feel great is because the parts of the body that are being used have thousands of nerve endings. Those nerve endings tell the brain what feels good and what doesn't. **Sex** can also release chemicals in the brain that can create feelings of happiness and relaxation. Everyone likes different things, and you get to choose what you want to do. Talking about likes and dislikes with a partner can help make sure **sex** is as enjoyable as possible.

The term "virgin" means different things to different people. ICYC defines **sex** as **oral**, **anal**, or **vaginal**. Because the term "virgin" does not have a medical definition, it is up to each person to define what **virginity** means for themselves. It's important to remember that no matter how a person defines "virginity," there is no shame in being a virgin or not being a virgin—each person's individual choice about sexuality is personal and normal. If someone chooses to have any type of **oral sex**, it's important to remember that, while **oral sex** cannot cause a **pregnancy**, it can spread **STIs**, so using **condoms** can help reduce that risk.

Well, what about a **tampon**? Again, ICYC defines **sex** as **oral**, **anal**, and **vaginal**. Using a **tampon** isn't a type of **sex**. If this answer doesn't match your understanding of **virginity**, that's okay, too. There are also other products a person can use if they are on their **period** and don't want to put anything inside their **vagina**.

IS IT OKAY TO HAVE SEX WITHOUT PROTECTION WITH YOUR HUSBAND OR WIFE

It doesn't matter what relationship status someone has—each person gets to decide if they want to use protection or not. If a person decides they no longer want to use protection, they need to talk to their partner about that decision. It is not okay to make a decision about stopping protection without telling your partner. Even when two people are married, they may choose to continue to use protection to avoid pregnancies or to protect against the transmission of STIs. Remember, some STIs cannot be cured, and that doesn't change after you get married! Other couples may choose to use protection off and on depending on whether they're ready for pregnancy. Each couple will need to talk about the risks and decide what works best for their relationship.

Masturbation is touching your own body because it feels good. Good news: you can't give yourself an **STI** or cause a **pregnancy** from **masturbation**! As a matter of fact, **masturbation** is a healthy activity many people choose to do. Some people do it and some don't. It's a person's choice whether they want to masturbate or not—and it often depends on their values, their body, and whether they feel comfortable doing it. If someone chooses to masturbate, it is important they do it in a private place.

Even if it's "like a lot," the act of **sex** or **masturbation** doesn't kill people. If someone dies during **sex** or while masturbating, it's usually because of other causes. A person can have **sex** or masturbate as much as they want, as long as it is consensual, doesn't get them in trouble, and doesn't get in the way of everyday life.

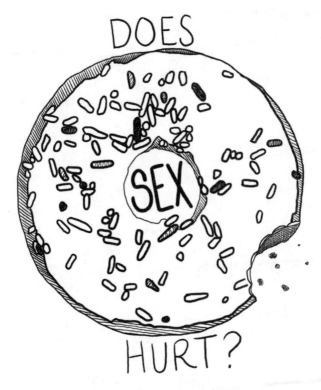

DOES SEX HURT?

Sex shouldn't hurt. If having **vaginal sex** for the first time, a person with a **vagina** may feel a pinching sensation, which sometimes happens if their **hymen** tears or stretches. If the person has already had **vaginal sex** before, or is having **anal sex**, and there is pain, it could be because there is an infection or an **STI**, because the person is not excited or relaxed enough, because there's not enough **lubricant**, or because of a medical condition. If **sex** hurts, it is important to stop and talk to your partner and/or your doctor. **Sex** should be pleasurable for both people.

SOME PEOPLE SAY THAT YOU BLEED WHEN YOU FIRST HAVE SEX, IS THAT TRUE? IF IT IS, DOES IT HAPPEN WITH EVERY WOMAN, OR ONLY SOME?

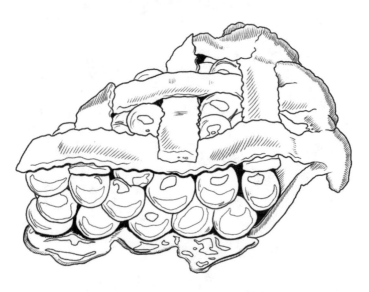

Everyone is different: some people with **vaginas** bleed during the first time they have **vaginal sex** and others don't. Both are perfectly normal. Bleeding can come from the **hymen** breaking/tearing for the first time. If someone does not bleed the first time they have **vaginal sex**, it does not mean they've had **sex** before. Many people's **hymens** break before they have **vaginal sex** for the first time.

what if my vagina leaks after sex?

After a person with a **vagina** has **sex**, it is common and normal for fluid to exit the **vaginal** opening. The fluids are normal **vaginal** fluids that are produced as a result of arousal. If a person with a **vagina** has had **sex** with a person with a **penis** and didn't use a **condom**, the **vaginal** fluids will be mixed with the ejaculated semen. Gravity then works its magic, and fluids in the **vagina** will come out. Even if this fluid comes out of the **vagina**, a **pregnancy** can still happen because the **sperm** may have already started swimming farther into the body.

HOW LONG SHOULD SEX LAST?

Sex can last as long as the people having **sex** want it to! Some people stop having **sex** after **orgasm** and/or **ejaculation**, and some people don't. It can take some people a short time to **orgasm** or ejaculate, and it can take others a long time. Some people will stop having **sex** even if they do not **orgasm** or ejaculate. Sexual activities might last a minute or an hour—it just depends on the person. The moment a person wants it to stop, **sex** should stop immediately.

HOW DO YOU MAKE A GIRL HORNY?

Sorry, but there's not just one way to make someone **horny** or turn them on. Everyone likes different things. For some people, this could be touching, things their partner says, or even looks and glances; other people set the mood with music or candles. The best way to know what turns them on is to ask them. It's important for both you and your partner to express yourselves, but also to listen to each other's boundaries.

An **orgasm** is a feeling of intense sexual pleasure, felt in the **genitals** or throughout the entire body. It is sometimes called "cumming" or **climaxing**. The **vagina** can release fluid and the **penis** can ejaculate **semen**, but not always. Some people say it feels like fireworks are going off. Don't worry, fireworks don't actually go off.

WHY DO GIRLS FAKE ORGASMS?

"Faking an **orgasm**" is when someone pretends to have an **orgasm** without actually having one. Anyone can do this, not just people with **vaginas**. People have different reasons why they might do this: they may be unable to **orgasm**, they may want to please their partner, they may feel ready to stop having **sex** because they're tired, or they may feel like that is what they are supposed to do. Whatever someone's reason, no one should feel like they have to fake an **orgasm**.

Open communication is super important in any sexual relationship. If someone doesn't speak up about what feels good and what doesn't, it could impact their ability to have **sex** they really enjoy.

WHY DO GUYS MOAN?

Here's the deal: have you ever said "Mmmmmm" when a delicious plate of food is put down in front of you? People react to enjoyable things in different ways, sometimes vocally. So, some people (of *every* **gender**) moan during **sex** or sexual

 activity. There isn't one reason for moaning—it could mean something feels really good, but it might mean something else. Honestly, the only way to know for sure why someone is moaning is to ask them.

WHAT IF THE *Penis* GETS STUCK IN THE *Vagina*?

Is it possible? Maybe. Is it likely? No. Let's talk about the **vagina**—it's like a pocket. Think about a pocket on a pair of jeans. When something is put inside, the pocket opens to hold it. Then when it is removed, the pocket lays back down flat. Same with the **vagina**. The **vaginal** walls stretch when a **penis** is inserted. When it comes out, the **vaginal** walls will go back again. The **vagina** is made of muscle, so it's meant to stretch! If someone is tense or nervous, the muscles of the **vagina** can contract; the **penis** may feel "stuck," but it can actually still come out. It cannot get "stuck" in the **vagina** forever.

*This is the same reason that **vaginas** don't get "loose" or gapped. The **vagina** is meant to stretch!*

If both people are cool with it, totally. It's medically okay to have **sex** during someone's **period**. It's a personal choice for both people involved. If someone has **sex** on their **period**, **pregnancy** and **STIs** are still possible. Using **condoms** and **birth control** can help reduce risk.

Put down the phone! You don't need to call poison control. **Semen** (**cum**) itself will not make someone sick—as in, it will not necessarily make someone's stomach ache. But, if someone has an **STI**, it can be spread through **oral sex**. **STIs** can make someone sick. Using a **condom** can help reduce that risk.

WILL MY TESTICLES EXPLODE IF I MASTURBATE TOO MUCH?

Relax, **testicles** do not explode. If a person is masturbating a lot, the **penis**, **testicles**, **vulva**, **clitoris**, or **vagina** can become sore to the touch or swollen. If **masturbation** is painful, it is a good idea to take a little break.

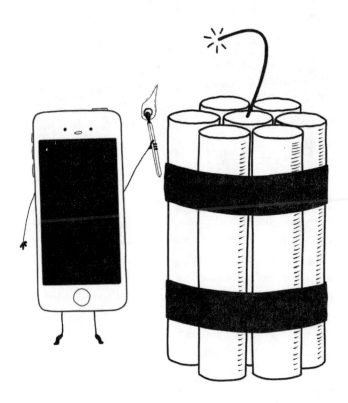

IS THE PINEAPPLE THING TRUE? DOES IT MAKE YOUR CUM TASTE BETTER?

There are a lot of myths out there about what **semen** tastes like. And even myths that some foods can change the taste of **semen**. But don't change your diet so fast. Eating a lot of pinapple doesn't make **semen** taste just like pineapple. There are some foods out there that can *slightly* change the way a person's body fluids taste or smell. However, it takes awhile for that change to happen, and there is no guarantee the change would be noticeable. In other words, don't count on it!

DO PEOPLE REALLY GET SLEEPY *After Sex?*

Yes, some people do get tired or sleepy after **sex**. Some people get sleepy during **sex**, and some people are already sleepy 30 minutes after they wake up in the morning! Everybody is different. Tiredness could be because **sex** felt like a work out, or because sexual release (**orgasm**) can make someone feel really relaxed afterwards. But other people may feel energized or even more excited after **sex**. Because **sex** can be different each time, people may feel some or all of these effects in their lifetime.

Lube, or lubrication, is typically used during **sex** to reduce friction and to increase sensation (or pleasure). If there is too much friction during **sex**, it can cause **condoms** to break or cause pain. Anybody can use **lube** to help make **sex** safer and feel better. If a person is going to use **lube**, it needs to be safe for the body. Water-based or silicone-based **lubricants** are often suggested. Do *not* use anything you find just because it's "slippery," like cooking oil, lotion, sunscreen, shampoo, etc.

*While most **condoms** come lubricated, water-based and silicone-based **lubes** are also safe for **condom** use. Oil-based **lubes** can break down the **condom** during use.*

WHEN SHOULD I START HAVING SEX (lose my virginity)?

We cannot tell you the best time to first have **sex.** Things that are important to consider before having **sex**: what do I want to protect against (**pregnancy, STIs**, or both); what protection method should we use; is my partner ready to have **sex**; do we feel comfortable talking about sexual boundaries; do I trust and respect my partner; what would we do about an **STI** or a **pregnancy;** and is it legal for people our age to have **sex** in our state? If you aren't able to answer all the things listed above, then you may not be ready to have safe and consensual **sex**. And everyone deserves to have safe and consensual **sex**.

WHAT'S PORN?

Porn, or **pornography**, is the name for videos or images that show nudity or sexual scenes. These images are only meant for adults, and buying or viewing them is illegal for anyone under eighteen years old. It's important to remember that **porn** is fiction, meaning that the people in **porn** videos are actors and the scenes aren't always realistic. Just like when a person sees an action movie with explosions or car chases, many of the things shown in **porn** aren't like real life.

DO YOU BURN CALORIES HAVING SEX OR MASTURBATING?

Would you believe that scientists have actually done some research on this? And they found that the answer is yes! Most people are surprised to learn that **sex** burns between one hundred and three hundred calories. But this depends on many things, like how long **sex** lasts, each person's weight, and how active it is. Masturbating typically burns fewer calories than **sex**.[4]

We show **love** in so many ways. Often TV or movies makes it seem like the only way to "prove" our **love** to someone is to have **sex**. But **love** is about trusting and respecting a person. **Love** is about supporting someone when they are having a hard time. **Love** can be holding hands until they get sweaty and still holding on. **Love** can be kissing until your lips get puffy. **Love** can be making each other laugh, and holding each other when you cry. **Love** is so much more than just **sex**.

CHAPTER TWO

"CAN YOU BREAK A PENIS?"

AND OTHER QUESTIONS ABOUT ANATOMY

TEXT "ICYC?" to 57890

SO WHAT'S, LIKE, A NORMAL PENIS SIZE?

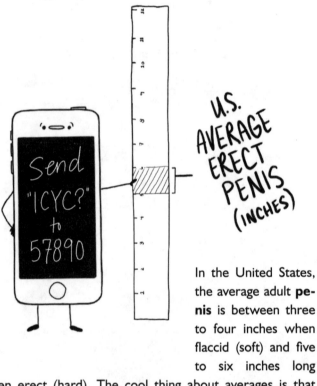

U.S. AVERAGE ERECT PENIS (INCHES)

In the United States, the average adult **penis** is between three to four inches when flaccid (soft) and five to six inches long when erect (hard). The cool thing about averages is that some people may be bigger and some people may be smaller. A lot of people worry about **penis** size. So it is important to remember everyone's body is different, and whatever your body looks like is normal and healthy for you, so try not to compare your body to others![5]

SHOULD MY VAGINA LOOK A CERTAIN WAY?

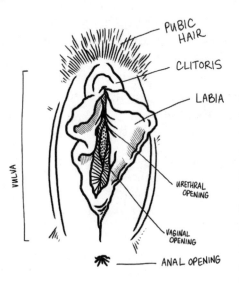

PUBIC HAIR

CLITORIS

LABIA

VULVA

URETHRAL OPENING

VAGINAL OPENING

ANAL OPENING

Many people say "**vagina**" when they're actually talking about the **vulva**. For people who have **vaginas**, the **vulva** is the outside part of the **genitals** that you can see, while the actual **vagina** is inside the body. There's no certain way any part of your **genitals** should look. In fact, **vaginas** and **vulvas** are as unique as faces—they all have the same parts, but everyone's looks a little different.

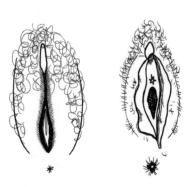

WHY ARE MY BOOBS UNEVEN?

Boobs are siblings, not identical twins! Just like every other part of the body, different people's **breasts** can grow differently. **Breasts** come in all different shapes and sizes, and a person's **breasts** may not always look exactly the same. It's common for one **breast** to be larger or smaller than the other, and one can even be a different shape.

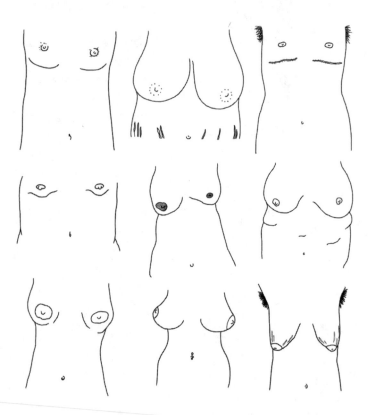

WHY DOES MY PENIS HAVE SOME EXTRA SKIN ON IT?

Extra skin around the head (top) of the **penis** is called foreskin. Some people have had their foreskin removed. This procedure is called **circumcision** and typically occurs soon after a baby is born. Families decide whether or not to circumcise the child, and this decision is made based on a number of reasons (religion, culture, family decision, etc.). If the foreskin remains on the **penis**, it is called "**intact**." Every **penis** is different, and both circumcised and **intact penises** are healthy and normal. If your **penis** has the foreskin, it will still work the same way as a **penis** without a foreskin. A person with their foreskin will need to practice self-care a little differently (like pulling the skin back when washing the **penis**), but other than that, the only difference is the way their **penis** looks. In all actuality, though, all **penises** look different from each other. Check out the drawing below for examples of what a **penis** can look like.

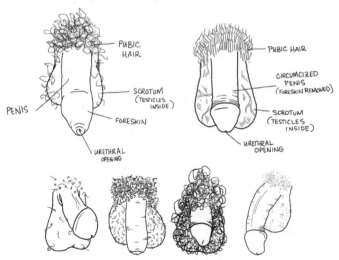

WHY DO ERECTIONS HAPPEN?

An **erection** is when the **penis** gets hard and stands away from the body. The **penis** is made up of **erectile tissue** (tissue that looks like a sponge). When a person gets sexually excited, it causes blood to flow into the **penis** and fill up the sponge-like material, which causes the material to expand and trap the blood. This causes the **penis** to grow bigger, feel hard, and stand up or out. Eventually the blood drains out of the **erectile tissue**. When this happens the **penis** will get soft again (flaccid) and lay back against the body.

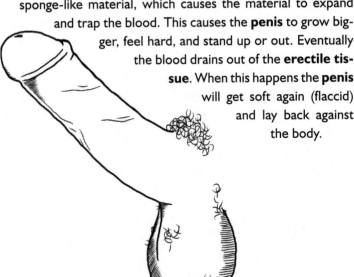

WHAT ARE BLUE BALLS AND CAN IT PERMANENTLY #%@$ YOU UP?

"**Blue balls**" is a term for when a person with a **penis** is sexually excited and has an **erection**, but isn't able to ejaculate. This sensation may feel heavy, uncomfortable, or even achy. The feeling does not last for long and will not have long term effects on the body (or **penis**!). A person does not have to ejaculate in order for the feeling or their **erection** to go away.

P.S. No matter who you are or how excited you are, it isn't okay to pressure your partner into having **sex** just because you are sexually aroused.

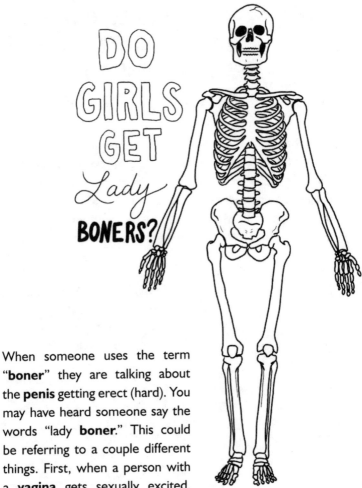

DO GIRLS GET Lady BONERS?

When someone uses the term "**boner**" they are talking about the **penis** getting erect (hard). You may have heard someone say the words "lady **boner**." This could be referring to a couple different things. First, when a person with a **vagina** gets sexually excited, blood will rush in and cause swelling to the clitoris, the **labia**, and the **vagina**. It is normal to feel a throbbing sensation when this happens. The clitoris may even feel hard. This term has also been used as slang when a person who identifies as a female is attracted to or turned on by another person.

HOW MANY EGGS DO I HAVE?

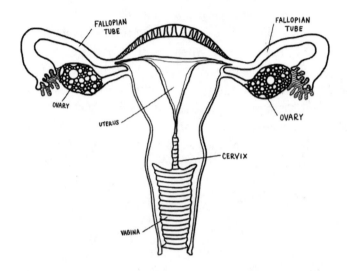

When a person with a **vagina** is born, they have all their **eggs**. They are typically born with 1-2 million **eggs** in their **ovaries**. Two million **eggs** is quite a birthday present. But don't worry, that doesn't mean there will be that many pregnancies. Many of the **eggs** will never fully develop or go anywhere outside of the **ovary**. A person with a **vagina** will likely release around 500 **eggs** during their lifetime, starting at **puberty** and ending at **menopause**.[6] (For more about what **menopause** is, head to page 59.)

WHERE IS SPERM MADE?

The **sperm** factory! Actually, it's the **testicles**, which will start making **sperm** when a person with a **penis** hits **puberty**. Thousands of **sperm** will be made every minute for the rest of their lives so, when you think about it, it *is* kind of like a **sperm** factory. Once the **sperm** have been made in the **testicles**, they move to the **epididymis**, which is just right upstairs from the **testicles**. They will hang out there for about two weeks until they are ready to be released, and if the **sperm** are not released during that time, they die and are reabsorbed by the body.[7]

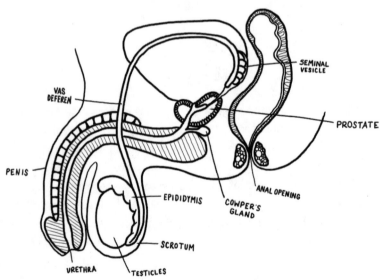

IF I GET WET DOWN THERE WHEN I SEE SOMEONE... DOES THAT MEAN I LIKE THEM?

No, that does not always mean that you like someone. It might, but it might not. When a person with a **vagina** feels sexually excited, the **vagina** may make more **vaginal** fluid and get "wetter." This is the body's natural response, which happens to create lubrication during **sex**. Similarly, if a person with a **penis** feels sexually excited, their **penis** may become erect (hard) and some **precum** (fluid produced by the body to clean out the **penis** prior to **ejaculation**) might come out, making that person's clothing a little wet. Although we might want to, we can't control who we're attracted to, but we do get to control what we do with those feelings. Just because your body has a normal physical response doesn't mean you have to act on that physical response. If you don't, nothing bad will happen. And that normal physical response doesn't necessarily mean you have a romantic interest in someone, or that you like them. It's also important to know that you can like someone, or be attracted to them, and *not* get wet. Everyone's body is different and reacts to being attracted to someone differently.

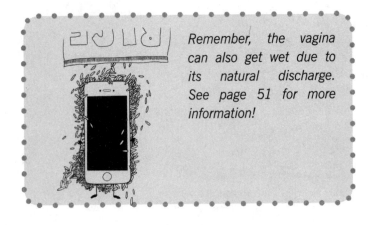

Remember, the vagina can also get wet due to its natural discharge. See page 51 for more information!

WHY DOES THE DOCTOR NEED TO SEE MY PRIVATES?

For the same reason they listen to your heart, a doctor needs to check a person's privates (**penis**, **scrotum**, **breasts**, **vulva**, and **vagina**) to make sure that they are healthy. It is still important that a doctor asks your permission before touching your private parts. A health care professional should also talk you through what they are doing and why. If you ever feel uncomfortable you can ask them to stop, and then you can talk with a parent or other trusted adult. Also, know that you can always have another person in the room with you if that helps you feel more comfortable. Speak up for yourself so that you feel good about getting the health care you deserve.

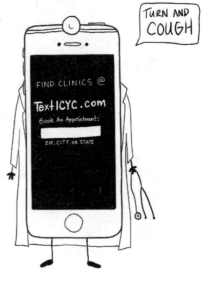

WHY DO MY BALLS HIDE WHEN I SWIM?

Trust us, it's not because they do not like water! Usually, when you go swimming, the water is *cold*! And your **testicles** don't like the cold. Whenever the **testicles** get cold, the **scrotum** (the skin or sack that holds the **testicles**) will pull them closer to the body to help keep them warm. This happens because the **testicles** need to be at a specific temperature so the body can produce **sperm** (and they are *always* making **sperm**). Think of the **scrotum** as your own personal heating and cooling system!

A person won't run out of **cum** (**semen** or ejaculate fluid). A person with a **penis** naturally starts making **sperm** and **semen** (**cum**) when they hit **puberty**, and they make it all day, every day from then on. As someone gets older, their production may slow down, but they will not run out. If a person ejaculates many times in a row, they may notice smaller amounts of fluid, but don't worry—the body will eventually make more.

*Did you know that even if a person with a **penis** doesn't have **testicles** (or has just one **testicle**) the body will still produce **semen** (**cum**)? That's because **semen** contains more than just **sperm**; fluids get added as the **sperm** is ready to leave the body. So even if there aren't actually **sperm** present, there is still the ejaculate fluid.*

WHAT DOES IT MEAN WHEN A GIRL SQUIRTS? DO ALL GIRLS DO THIS?

Squirting is when someone with a **vagina** releases fluid from their **urethra** during **sexual arousal** or when they're really turned on. This is different from peeing. It may happen when they **orgasm**, or not. Some people do it and others don't. Both are healthy and normal.

Nope, the **vagina** does not fart. Sometimes air gets trapped in the **vagina**, which can make a fart-like noise when released, but while the sound might be the same, that's where the silimarities end. A fart is gas made from digested food in the stomach and intestines (digestive system). The **vagina** is part of the reproductive system, so gas or air cannot actually be created in the **vagina**. How the air gets inside the **vagina** can vary, and yes, it can happen when something gets inserted into the **vagina**. Often people call the sound made by air escaping the **vagina** a "**queef**."

HOW DEEP CAN A PENIS GO IN A VAGINA?

This depends on the **vagina**. From the opening of the **vagina** to the cervix (the gateway between the **vagina** and the **uterus**), the **vagina** is, on average, about three to four inches deep. You can think of the **vagina** like a pocket: most of the time it stays closed, but when something is put inside, the **vagina** stretches to make room to fit what's going inside. But no matter how deep a **vagina** is, a **penis** won't get past the cervix. Just because the **vagina** can stretch doesn't mean it has to. If something feels uncomfortable or hurts, it could mean the **vagina** is stretching too much. It's important to talk to a partner about what feels good and what doesn't. If something doesn't feel good, stop the behavior and consider talking to a **health care provider**.

WHAT DO SPERM LOOK LIKE?

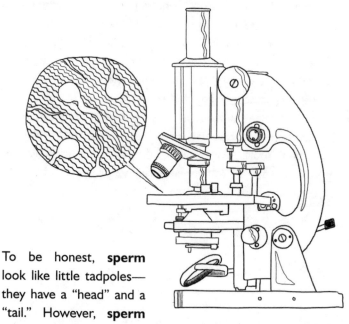

To be honest, **sperm** look like little tadpoles— they have a "head" and a "tail." However, **sperm** are incredibly tiny and can only be seen under a microscope. The fluid they travel in is called **semen**, which consists of the **sperm** and nutrients that keep the **sperm** healthy and alive. **Semen** (or **cum**) is the fluid that is released during **ejaculation**. **Semen** often comes out as a clear or white fluid and can be sticky to touch.

CAN YOU BREAK A PENIS?

The answer is yes and no. Confusing, right? The **penis** does not have a bone in it, so it cannot break like someone's leg would break. But if the **penis** bends too far or is injured while it is erect, it can cause a "penile fracture," which can be painful and may need medical attention. When this happens, the person might hear a popping sound, caused by the spongy **erectile tissue** bursting. This injury can only happen when the **penis** is erect because when the **penis** is soft, or flaccid, it can bend more easily. Injury to the **penis**, though not common, is more likely to happen during **vaginal sex**, **anal sex**, or aggressive **masturbation**.

DON'T YOU PEE OUT OF THE VAGINA?

A lot of people think this! But the truth is that a person with a **vagina** pees out of their **urethral** opening, which is a tiny hole above their **vaginal** opening. The **vaginal** opening is where menstrual blood, **vaginal** discharge, and a baby may leave the body. The **urethral** opening is hooked up to your **bladder** and is part of the system that eliminates waste from your body, while the **vaginal** opening is connected to the reproductive system. So, there are two separate holes there! But even though there are two holes down there, there is no way you will get them confused because the **urethral** opening is super small. There is no way a **tampon**, finger, **penis**, **sex** toy, or anything else can "accidently" go in the **urethral** opening.

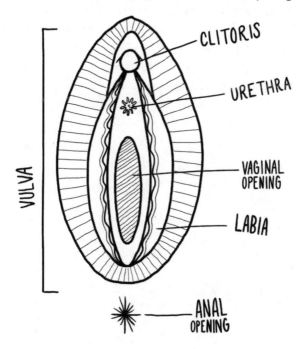

CLITORIS

URETHRA

VAGINAL OPENING

LABIA

VULVA

ANAL OPENING

what does **POPPING** *your* *Cherry mean?*

"Popping the cherry" is slang for "breaking" the **hymen**. The **hymen** is a very thin membrane that partly covers the opening to the **vagina**. Sometimes when a person with a **vagina** has **vaginal sex** for the first time, their **hymen** may tear or stretch, and they may notice a pinching sensation and a small amount of blood. However, a person does not always bleed the first time they have **sex** because the **hymen** may have already torn earlier in life, or because the **hymen** hasn't torn but is instead stretching.

Other ways the **hymen** can "break":
▸ Horseback riding
▸ Gymnastics
▸ Riding a bike
▸ Inserting a tampon

WHAT'S THE *white stuff* IN MY UNDERWEAR?

During and after **puberty**, people with **vaginas** may notice a white or clear fluid in their underwear. This is typically called **vaginal** discharge. **Vaginal** discharge is how the **vagina** keeps itself clean. It is totally normal and healthy. Sometimes a person may notice that throughout their **menstrual cycle** it may change in texture and amount. If it ever changes color (like turns green or yellow), becomes chunky in texture, starts to smell different, or causes itching, they should go see a healthcare provider.

Since the **vagina** is self cleaning, no fancy soaps or **douches** are needed—they actually do more harm than good. Douching can wash away all of the bacteria, including the good bacteria that works to keep the **vagina** healthy. Say no to douching!

HOW OLD ARE YOU WHEN YOU HAVE TO GET YOUR VAGINA CHECKED?

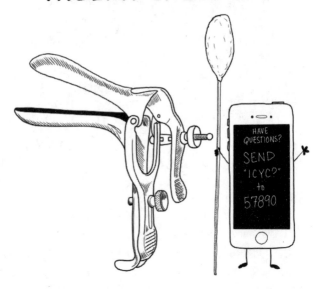

People should regularly look at their own **genitals**, so they know what is normal and will notice a change if one happens. This doesn't have to be a big deal—just take a quick look before getting in the shower. There are special checkups called **pap smears** that people with **vaginas** should start getting around the age of twenty-one. This procedure checks the cells of the cervix for cancer. If you're feeling pain in or around your **genitals**, or if you think something is wrong, you should see a **health care provider** regardless of your age. For people with a **penis**, your doctor will check your **penis** and **testicles** yearly. They are feeling for any lumps and making sure your **genitals** are developing at the same pace as the rest of your body.

CAN MY CLITORIS GO MISSING AS I AGE?

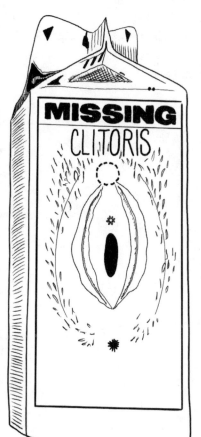

Good news: just like any other part of a body, the **clitoris** might change or feel different as a person gets older, but it does not disappear with age (because it is attached!). All people are born with skin that covers the **clitoris** (**clitoral hood**), and this can make the **clitoris** harder to see on some bodies. Some people with a **clitoris** also report that the sensitivity of the nerve endings change as they age. This can be a normal part of aging, and every body is different.

CAN A BEAR SMELL PERIOD BLOOD?

A bear does have a strong sense of smell, and it's likely a bear can smell blood. But research says that a bear will not attack someone because they are on their **period**. Bears are much more interested in the smell of food than in the smell of pads.[8]

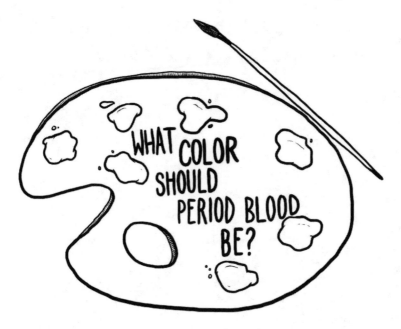

While it might be cool if **period** blood were green and glittery, it's still blood, so it's gonna fall in the red category. **Period** blood can change depending on where you are in your **menstrual cycle**. It can be anywhere from dark brown and almost black to a rusty or even bright red. It is important for you to know your body and what is normal for you. If your **period** blood changes or seems unusual, it is okay to ask someone like a parent or **health care provider**.

DO BREASTS ALWAYS HAVE MILK IN THEM?

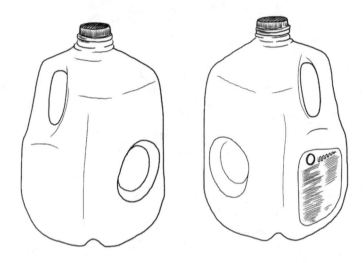

No, **breasts** do not always have milk in them. The duct system that helps the **breasts** make milk starts developing during **puberty**. Even though a person's **breasts** can make milk, they don't usually start creating milk until they become pregnant, and typically not until the fifth month of **pregnancy**. It's important to know that sometimes the **breasts** can leak a clear fluid even when a person isn't pregnant. This fluid is usually normal, but if this is new then it's always a good idea to check in with your doctor.[9]

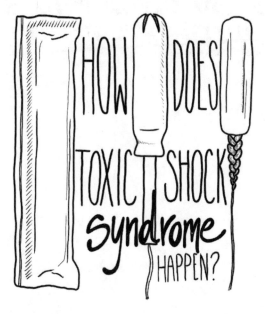

Toxic Shock Syndrome (TSS) is a rare blood infection. One way it can happen is by leaving a **tampon** in the **vagina** much longer than recommended (read the instructions on the **tampon** box to know how long it can be worn). Signs of TSS are similar to the flu and can include high fever, vomiting, drop in blood pressure, diarrhea, and rash. If a person thinks they have TSS, it's important they remove the **tampon** and go to a doctor immediately.

DO YOU CLEAN PENISES WITH EXTRA SKIN DIFFERENTLY?

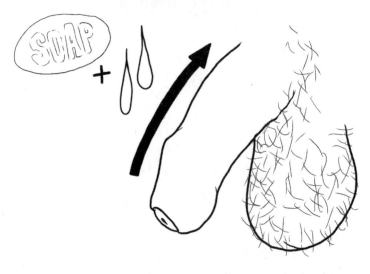

People with foreskin are referred to as having an **intact penis**. The way they care for their **penis** is different from the self-care routine of a person who has been circumcised (a person whose foreskin was removed). Everyone needs to clean their **penis**, and a person with an **intact penis** needs to simply roll back the foreskin to wash the head of the **penis**, using warm water and soap. This is necessary because bacteria can get trapped and build up between the foreskin and the top of the **penis**.

HOW OLD ARE YOU WHEN YOU GET MENOPAUSE?

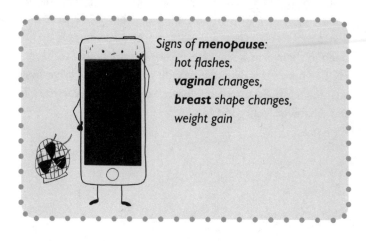

So what is **menopause** in the first place? **Menopause** is when a person's body stops having a **period**, stops releasing **eggs**, and greatly reduces the production of reproductive **hormones** (**estrogen**, **progesterone**, and **testosterone**). In the United States, the average age a person with a **vagina** starts **menopause** is 51. But it isn't uncommon for **menopause** to start as early as 48 or as late as 55.[10]

Signs of **menopause**:
hot flashes,
vaginal changes,
breast shape changes,
weight gain

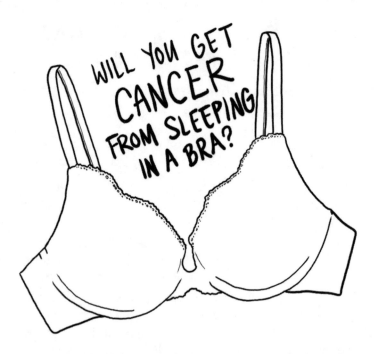

Nope! Bras can be uncomfortable, supportive, itchy, pokey, pretty, ugly, and so many other things, but there is no evidence that sleeping in one causes cancer. Many people do not sleep in their bras because it is more comfortable to have it off. But here's the deal, everybody gets to decide what feels best for them. So take it off, leave it on, do whatever you like and whatever feels good to you![11]

Usually, when people ask this question they are asking about **penis** size. And here's the deal with **penis** size: everybody's **penis** is different. **Penises** can be smaller, bigger, wider, longer, shorter, or in-between. Whether or not it "matters" often refers to whether or not a partner prefers a certain **penis** size. Some people may prefer a bigger **penis** and some may prefer a smaller **penis** and some may not care at all. For many people, getting turned on is about much more than the size of their partner's **penis**. It's important to know that a person can't change the size of their **penis**. So it's not okay to make someone feel bad about their body. And no matter what size a **penis** is, they all work the same way.

CAN TAMPONS GET LOST IN THE VAGINA?

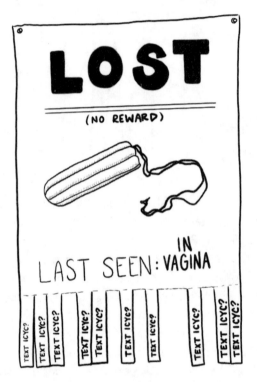

Many people think of the **vagina** as a deep, dark, mysterious, never-ending tunnel. Well, that is just not true! The front of the **vagina** is called the **vaginal** opening and the back or end point is called the **cervix**. The opening of the **cervix** is so tiny that only menstrual blood and **sperm** can get through, so it keeps a **tampon** and anything else that goes into the **vagina** from going farther into the body. The **tampon** will not get lost because the **cervix** is standing guard (thanks **cervix**!). So don't worry—the **tampon** will be there.

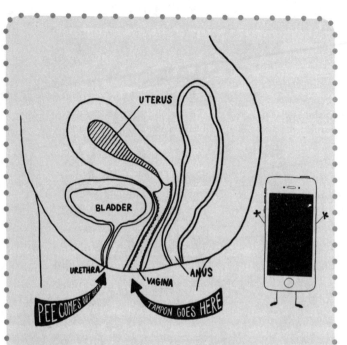

And while we're at it—let's talk about peeing and **tampons**. The **tampon** is in the **vagina**. Pee leaves the body through the **urethra** (a hole above the **vagina**). So, guess what, a person can pee and have a **tampon** in at the same time!!

IS IT NORMAL FOR BOOBS TO HURT?

Oh boobs, most of the time they just hang there…but some-times they ache, itch, get in the way, feel tingly, or even feel good. It is common for **breasts** to hurt. They can hurt dur-ing **puberty** because they are growing. They can ache before or during a person's **period** because the **hormones** in the body are changing. They can ache after wearing a bra all day. If the **breasts** have severe pain or pain every day, ask a doc-tor about it.

CAN YOU HAVE A PENIS AND A VAGINA?

A person cannot have a fully functional **penis** and a fully functional **vagina**, but it is possible for a person to be **intersex**. Being **intersex** means that someone's **sex** characteristics (how they look and what makes their body work in certain ways) can include a variety of different chromosomes, **genitals**, **reproductive organs**, or **hormones**. This can be really different for every **intersex** person. Some differences might be noticeable at birth, whereas other differences might not show up until later (like during **puberty**), or only show up with special tests.[12]

IS IT NORMAL FOR NIPPLES TO BE HAIRY?

Hair, hair, everywhere! Yep, even **nipples**! Just like other body hair, some people may grow hair around their **nipples**, while others might not. It might be thicker and darker than their other body hair or it might be lighter and fuzzy. It is nothing to be embarrassed about if you have hair around your **nipples**. Just like with other hair, a person can choose to leave it alone or remove it.

WHY ARE TESTICLES OUTSIDE THE BODY?

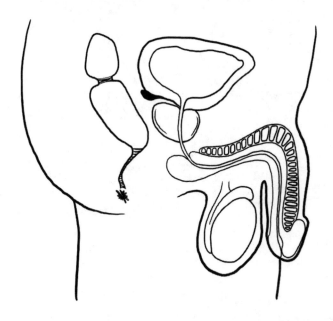

Do you remember the story of *Goldilocks and the Three Bears*? Goldilocks kept trying the porridge, and one bowl was too hot, another was too cold, but the last bowl was just right. Well, **sperm** are a little like that—they have to be made at just the right temperature to survive. The **testicles** hang outside of the body, in the **scrotum**, in order to stay at the right temperature to make **sperm**. If they were inside the body, the **sperm** might get a little too hot.

Where is the **G SPOT?**

Ah, the G-spot! Some people believe it is a myth, and some believe it is a magic button. The **G-spot** is an area one to three inches inside the **vagina**, towards the belly button, that has lots of nerve endings. For some people, having this spot touched feels good (and can cause an **orgasm**), and for others, there might not be much sensation at all. When it comes to what feels good, each person is different, and that's okay! The **G-spot** is short for the Gräfenberg spot, named after the doctor that started the research. But it was introduced to the world by Dr. Beverly Whipple.

CHAPTER THREE

"DO GUYS REALLY CUM IN THEIR SLEEP?"

AND OTHER QUESTIONS ABOUT PUBERTY

WHY DO GIRLS AND BOYS FLIRT WITH EACH OTHER AND ACT WEIRD AROUND EACH OTHER?

The stuttering, the blushing, the wondering where to put your hands! It can be really weird to watch people flirt, especially if it's new for them. People flirt for different reasons. During **puberty**, **hormones** are being released in the body that can make people feel romantic or have sexual feelings they may never have felt before. Some people choose to act on these feelings (flirt, ask someone out, hold hands, kiss) and some people choose not to do anything at all. It is also common for people to feel nervous or even "weird" around someone they like because they may not know what to say, may be worried about saying the wrong thing, or may not know what they want to happen.

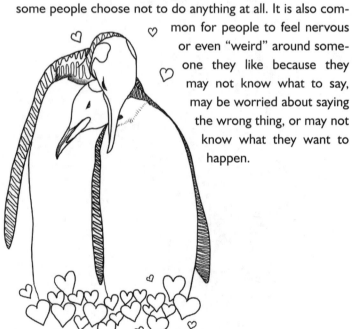

No matter what the age, its not weird at all. People can have sexual feelings at any time throughout their lives and can experience them in many different ways. Often, these feelings get stronger once someone goes through **puberty**, but everyone is different. There is nothing wrong with having sexual feelings or not having sexual feelings. It's what someone chooses to do with these feelings that is important. Some people choose to ignore them, some people choose to talk about them, some people choose to touch their own bodies, and if both people agree, some people choose to be sexual with each other. Only do what you feel comfortable doing.

It's not just sexual feelings that will change during **puberty**— it's possible for  all of your feelings to change. You may not feel as close to the people you used to, or you might bounce back and forth between liking and disliking people. Your emotions may feel like a rollercoaster, but don't worry, they will even out over time.

Totally, and it's nothing to be embarrassed about. During **puberty**, it is common for the **penis** to get erect (hard) and ejaculate while a person sleeps. This is called a **wet dream**. It can happen to some people a lot, and might never happen to other people. A **wet dream** can happen when a person is dreaming about anything; it does not have to be something sexually exciting. When having a **wet dream**, a person is not peeing, even though the bed might be wet. They are actually releasing **semen**. Most people grow out of this in time.

WHY DO I KEEP BREAKING OUT?

Breaking out usually refers to acne, pimples, or zits. Acne can be common during **puberty** because during this time people produce lots of **hormones**, which can make their skin more oily. Acne doesn't come from someone being dirty or

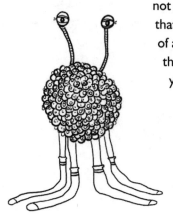

not washing. However, one thing that can help reduce the amount of acne a person gets is cleaning their face regularly. Washing your face cleans out the pores and gets rid of extra oil. If you are concerned about acne, talk to a doctor.

WHAT AM I SUPPOSED TO DO WITH MY PUBIC HAIR?

Guess that depends on what you want to do with it—you do you! **Pubic hair** can help keep the **genitals** safe and protected. Some people choose to remove their **pubic hair** by waxing, trimming, or shaving, but keeping it is also a great option. Whatever someone does with their **pubic hair** is their decision. They should choose whatever makes them feel best. And remember, if someone chooses to remove their **pubic hair**, it's important to know that the skin in the pubic area is sensitive, so they should talk to an adult for advice before trying to remove it.

Puberty doesn't happen overnight! Instead, think of **puberty** more as a journey. **Puberty** is a time when a person's body changes from looking like a child's body to looking like an adult's body. This can start to happen between the ages of eight and sixteen and can last for a few years. Some changes will be quick, and some might take longer. Everyone's body is different. If any of the changes feel hard to deal with, find a supportive adult to talk to.

WHY HAVEN'T I GOTTEN BOOBS YET? MY SISTER'S ARE HUGE!

It's important to remember that everyone's body is different. And all bodies are great, whether they have big boobs, small boobs, or no boobs. It is possible you will have **breasts** (boobs) the same size as your sister's, but it is also possible that your **breasts** will be smaller or bigger than hers. **Breasts** grow during **puberty** (often between the ages of 8 and 16), but they can change throughout a person's life. For example, if a person gains or loses a lot of weight, or gets pregnant, their breasts may change in size. People can't control when their boobs grow or how big they will get.

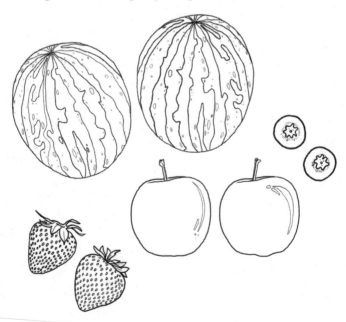

WHY DON'T BOYS GET PERIODS?

The simple answer? It's all about anatomy! People with **penises** don't get **periods** because they don't have a **uterus**. A **period** happens when the **uterus** sheds its lining.

*The term "boy" refers to **gender**. If someone has a **uterus** and identifies as a boy, they can get their **period**. See chapter 4 for more information on gender.*

send us questions by texting "ICYC?" to 57890

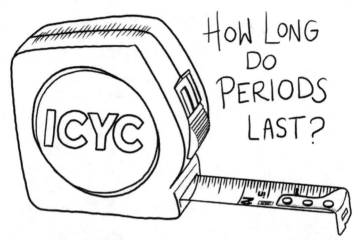

HOW LONG DO PERIODS LAST?

ICYC

Don't worry, it's not forever! It's normal to bleed anywhere from two to seven days during a **period**. The full **menstrual cycle** lasts from the first day of a **period** to the first day of the next **period**. The average **menstrual cycle** is about twenty-five to thirty days, but it can be as short as twenty-one days or longer than thirty-five—it's different for each person. The number of days in a person's cycle may also vary from month to month.[13] People with **vaginas** start having their **periods** during **puberty**, and will continue having **periods** until they go through **menopause**. (For more on **menopause** go to page 59.)

WHY ARE GIRLS SO MOODY ON THEIR PERIODS?

Especially during **puberty**, everyone (no matter their **gender**) goes through emotional cycles because of **hormones**. For people with **vaginas**, they may experience these hormonal changes each month in the days or weeks before they start their **periods**. Some people may feel sad, grumpy, irritable, hungry, tired, or many other emotions; while other people may not have a noticeable change in their mood at all. But remember, just because someone's feeling moody, it doesn't always have to do with their **period**. They could just be having a bad day, or they could be sick of being asked, "Are you on your **period**?"

Some people may notice cravings, like for certain foods, while on their **period**. Despite what people think, craving chocolate isn't a result of **hormones**. People usually crave the things that give them comfort because **periods** don't always feel great.

DON'T ASK!

WHAT CAN SOMEONE USE IF THEY ARE ON THEIR PERIOD?

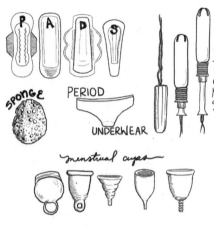

So many options! There are lots of products to help keep the blood from getting on your clothes. Some people use pads, which stick on the underwear to catch blood as it comes out of the **vagina**. Some people use **tampons**, which are inserted into the **vagina** to absorb blood. People can also use **menstrual cups** or specially designed sponges, which are inserted into the **vagina** to hold the blood, and which can be reused. There is even special underwear that helps absorb the blood. With so many options, it's important to figure out what works for you and your lifestyle.

You can find directions on how to use each of these options on the packaging.

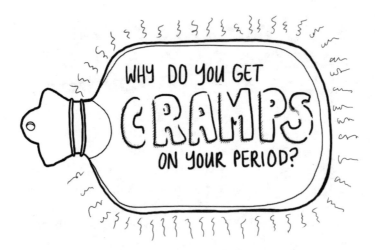

WHY DO YOU GET **CRAMPS** ON YOUR PERIOD?

A person gets cramps because the **uterus** is contracting to release menstrual blood. Some people have mild or no cramps, and some people have intense cramps. While cramping can be normal, it should not be so painful that it gets in the way of your ability to do what you usually do. If your **period** cramps are extra painful or last a really long time, it's important to talk with a doctor. Some good ways to relieve cramps are: taking a hot bath, taking **over-the-counter** pain medication, stretching or exercising, or using a heating pad.

WHEN YOU HAVE A TINGLY FEELING IN YOUR PENIS, WHAT SHOULD YOU DO?

A tingling feeling can be different things: an itch, the sensation of needing to pee, or sexual **excitement**. If a person with a **penis** is getting sexually excited, the **penis** might get erect (or hard). This can make the **penis** stand up and away from the body. A person can choose to do nothing, and the **erection** will go away (after time, the **penis** will get soft and lay against the body again). A person could choose to touch the **penis**, but this should only be done in private. Or a person might choose to be sexual with another person, as long as both people give permission (consent).

WHY DO I SOMETIMES WAKE UP WITH AN ERECTION? (morning wood)

Well, good morning! Getting an **erection** during sleep or when waking up in the morning is normal and healthy. This is especially common when going through **puberty**, but can happen at any age. There are different theories why this happens. The two most common theories are: because the body is most relaxed in the morning or, because there are higher amounts of **hormones** in the morning. Just because a person wakes up with an **erection** doesn't mean they were dreaming about something sexy.[14]

WHAT DO I DO IF I DON'T WANT PUBERTY TO HAPPEN?

Ready or not, you can't hide from **puberty**. **Puberty** is a time in life when people go through many changes, and these changes are physical, emotional, and social. Everyone feels differently about **puberty** and the changes the body is going through, especially when it is happening to *their* body. **Puberty** starts and ends at different times for different people, and it is a very individual experience. With all these changes, some people are excited and like the idea of going through **puberty**, while others get worried or anxious about the idea. One way to handle all the emotions and changes is to discuss what you are feeling with someone you trust.

WILL I REALLY GROW HAIR EVERYWHERE?

Although there is *a lot* of hair that starts growing during **puberty**, do not fear—it will not grow *everywhere*! Most people will grow thicker, darker hair on their legs. Hair will begin to grow under the arms and in the pubic area (on the **vulva**, the **scrotum**, and the area around the **penis**). Some people might start to grow hair on their chest and face. Wow, that does seem like everywhere! But here's the cool thing: your body is your own. You get to decide what to do with the new hair. Some people leave it and let it grow, some shave it or wax it, and some people even dye it different colors. Whatever you decide to do with your hair is your choice.

Don't worry, you can't catch **puberty**! It's not a cold, it's a set of physical, emotional, and social changes that happen over time. It might seem like everyone is going through **puberty** at the same time, but that's only because everyone goes through **puberty** at around the same age (usually between the ages of eight and sixteen). Everyone's body is different, and **puberty** will start whenever the body is ready. Even though **puberty** is not contagious, it does happen to everyone. So hold on—it is a fun and wild ride.

Did you know? Hands and feet growing are often the first signs **puberty** *has started!*[15]

CAN YOU PUT A TAMPON IN YOUR BUTT?

Can you? Sure. Is that what they are meant for? No. **Tampons** are meant to be put in the **vagina** to collect **period** blood. You should never insert something into the anus/butt that isn't meant to go there. Inserting something into the butt that is not meant to go in the butt can be harmful and dangerous to the body.

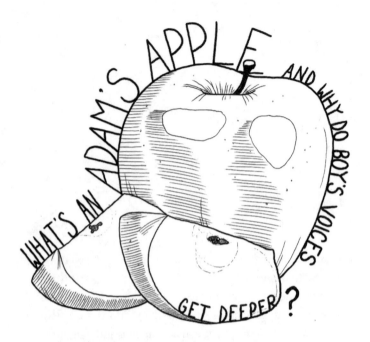

The "Adam's Apple" is a bump that sticks out on the front of the neck. It's not something stuck in the throat—it's actually the larynx, or voice box, which is located in the throat and gives you your voice. During **puberty**, the larynx grows larger, usually becoming more noticeable in people with **penises**. This growth and expansion of the muscles is what causes some people's voices to get deeper during **puberty**.[16]

WHEN WILL I BE FULLY GROWN?

"Is someone ever truly fully grown?" Sorry, we went a little deep there! Growing up means different things to different people. If we are thinking about a person's body developing into adulthood, this is one way people "grow up," and it is called **puberty**. **Puberty** is a time when a person's body changes from looking like a child's body to looking like an adult's body. This typically starts between the ages of eight and sixteen and usually includes at least one big growth spurt. But **puberty** can take many years, so depending on when someone starts **puberty**, it may be years before a person is "fully grown." Being fully grown doesn't just refer to a person's body, but it can also refer to brain development. Did you know that a person's brain isn't fully developed until twenty-five-years-old? Being fully grown takes time and looks different for everyone.

CHAPTER FOUR

"IS TWELVE TOO YOUNG TO KNOW I'M BI?"

AND OTHER QUESTIONS ABOUT SEXUAL ATTRACTION, SEXUAL ORIENTATION, GENDER IDENTITY, AND GENDER EXPRESSION

WHAT IS GENDER, ORIENTATION, AND EXPRESSION, ANYWAY?

The Trans Student Educational Resources center created this graph to help people understand gender. And who doesn't love a unicorn (especially an inclusive, educational unicorn!)?[17]

Gender is the way someone feels inside and how they identify themselves. Some examples of how people identify are: woman, man, **gender fluid**, and **queer.** But there are many other ways in which people can identify. **Gender** expression can refer to how someone expresses themselves. Like, how someone dresses, styles their hair, or behaves. A person's **gender identity** and **gender** expression can be different from each other or the same. It's important to be respectful and not make assumptions about how people identify. **Sexual orientation** refers to who someone is attracted to. Attraction can be physical, based on how someone looks or the body parts they have, but can also be emotional, based on who they like spending time with. Some people might identify themselves as **gay**, **lesbian**, **straight**, or **bisexual**. Check out the Gender Unicorn, from TSER, that helps visually break down these differences.

HOW DO YOU BECOME THE OTHER GENDER?

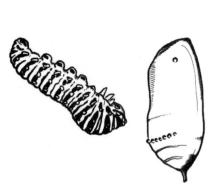

When people are born, their sex is recorded at birth, based on if they have a penis or a vagina. The way a person feels inside is their gender. For some people, their sex recorded at birth feels comfortable or right for them. and for some people, it doesn't feel right or comfortable. If someone feels their sex recorded at birth is not right for them, they might take steps towards affirming their gender, this can be called transitioning. People whose gender identity is different from their sex recorded at birth may identify as transgender, while others may not. Transitioning can be social (how a person dresses) and/ or medical (medicine or surgery) and can be very different for each and every person. The truth is that there's no right way to transition! No matter how a person identifies or how they express their gender, it is important to respect their identity. If someone needs support around transitioning, it can help to talk to an adult they trust. Check out the Wrap up section for more information and resources. Isn't it cool that you can identify however you want and make changes that feel right for you.

WAIT, YOU'RE TELLING ME THERE ARE MORE THAN TWO GENDERS?

Ah, the age-old question we ask every new parent: blue or pink, boy or girl? Honestly, there are many different beliefs about how many **genders** *actually* exist. Sometimes people may be more familiar with the binary two **genders**, male and female, while others agree there are unlimited **gender** possibilities. A person's **gender identity** can be any of the following and more: woman, man, **intersex**, **gender queer**, **gender fluid**, or **gender nonconforming**. In the end, though, it doesn't really matter how many **genders** there actually are—just that you respect how others identify themselves, and they respect how you identify yourself! Check out page 96 (**gender** unicorn) for more information on **gender**.

HOW DO YOU BECOME GAY/BI/LESBIAN?

Sexual orientation is not a choice. **Sexuality** is a lifelong process, starting with understanding yourself and leading to understanding who you are attracted to. Sometimes **sexual orientation** changes over time, and sometimes it stays the same. **Sexual orientation** cannot be changed with therapy, treatment, or pressure from family or friends. Each person defines their own **sexual orientation**.[18]

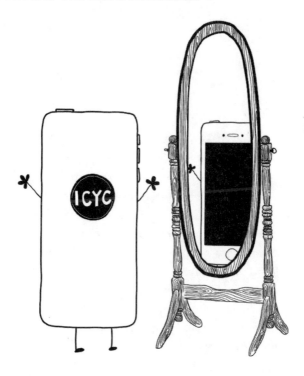

Not at all! People can know their orientation, or who they like, at any age. "**Bisexual**" refers to a person who is attracted to two genders. As people go through **puberty**, they often start to notice who they are and aren't attracted to. They may notice that they get butterflies in their stomach when that cute boy from math class walks past, or that their cheeks become rosy when they watch a movie starring their favorite actress. Sometimes people may tell you things like, "You're just confused" or "You're just experimenting." But honestly, you know yourself best—and only you know how you identify and who you're attracted to. Some people know their attraction and **sexual orientation** right away, and others may need some time to explore it.

HOW DO I KNOW IF MY FRIEND LIKES GIRLS TOO?

Wouldn't it be so cool if we had special gadgets to tell us to whom someone is attracted to? Unfortunately, we can't ever know who someone is attracted to unless they tell us. You get to decide if you want to share your **sexual orientation** with your friends. But just because you share your **sexual orientation**, it does not mean they have to share that information with you. Your friend might feel comfortable telling you, or they might not. It's their own decision as to who they decide to tell, so it's important to respect their feelings.

I HAVE A CRUSH ON MY STRAIGHT FRIEND! WHAT DO I DO?

It can be really tough having a crush on a friend. And honestly, this may be true no matter what their **sexual orientation** is. It can be hard to know exactly how to act around them or how to feel towards them. And it can be especially hard to figure out how they feel towards you. Whenever this happens, you have some options for how to handle the situation. You may decide to tell your friend how you feel, or you may decide to keep your feelings private. But it's important to know that people can't change to whom they are attracted to. So if your friend expresses that they don't feel the same way towards you, you need to respect their feelings. It might also be helpful to talk with them about how you both can feel comfortable in your friendship moving forward.

Why not? Only you can decide how (and if) you identify your **sexual orientation**. Who you date, or even who you have **sex** with, does not have to determine your **sexual orientation**. Dating a new person won't change your orientation unless you want it to.

WHY ARE PRONOUNS SO IMPORTANT?

A person's pronouns can often help communicate their **gender** to others. Some people might use the pronouns "he/him," others might use "she/her," and others might use "they/them." They know themselves best, so only they can say which pronouns are right for them. Being mis-**gendered** (meaning being addressed as a **gender** outside of the one you identify with) can often be hurtful. To be respectful of a person's **gender** and validate their identity, it's important to use the pronouns that they ask you to use. Using the correct pronouns can help everyone feel safe and respected—and is not that hard!

HOW DO I KNOW IF SOMEONE IS GAY?

The only way to know if someone is **gay** is for them to tell you themselves! You can't tell someone's **sexual orientation** by the way they look, act, or talk. A lot of people will make assumptions, but you cannot tell who someone is attracted to by any of those things. And really, do we even need to know? A person's **sexual orientation** is their own business, and if they feel like disclosing it, they will.

*How do I know if someone is **trans**?*
▶ *Just like with **sexual orientation**, the only way to know if someone is **transgender** is for them to tell you. You can't tell someone's **gender** by the way they look, act, or talk.*

I DON'T REALLY UNDERSTAND WHY SEX IS SUCH A BIG DEAL. I DON'T REALLY HAVE THE URGE TO BE SEXUAL. IS THAT OK?

Heck yeah! Everybody has a different level of sexual desire. Some people have a lot, some people only feel desire after getting to know another person really, really well, and some people don't have any sexual desire at all. All of those are okay, normal, and healthy. Some people want a romantic relationship but do not want a sexual relationship. Often, people who don't feel sexual feelings or desires identify as asexual, or **Ace**.

DO I HAVE TO TELL MY FAMILY I'M A LESBIAN?

Not necessarily! The decision of whether to tell people about your **sexual orientation** (**coming out**) is one that **LGBTQ+** people will make often, not just once. So it is a decision you will likely make over and over again throughout your life in many different situations. Some situations may be easier than others, and some may take more thought. People might choose to tell their whole family, or they might choose one or two people to tell first (like a favorite cousin or a sibling). Whether or not you tell your family may depend on your family's culture, beliefs, and level of support, as well as whether you feel safe with them. This is a personal decision, and only you get to decide if, when, and how you do it.[19]

HOW DO I SUPPORT A FRIEND THAT IS GAY?

How do you support any friend? You listen to them. You try to understand what they are going through. You let them know that you care for them. Everyone deserves to be accepted for who they are. And hey, it might even help to ask them what they need! Different people need different things to feel **loved** and supported. Don't forget it helps to show support in front of other people too. Sometimes people who feel like they always have to defend themselves can use a friend to speak up with/for them.

WHY do PEOPLE USE the TERM PARTNER

INSTEAD OF BOYFRIEND OR GIRLFRIEND?

There's not just one reason. Some people feel like it is more inclusive, because the word "partner" can refer to a person of any **gender identity** or **sexual orientation**. Some people use the term "partner" so that they don't have to **out** their **sexual orientation** when they talk about their romantic partner. And some people feel like the term better represents their relationship. Always make sure to let someone else define their relationship and use the term that feels best for them.

WHAT'S THE DIFFERENCE BETWEEN HETERONORMATIVITY AND HETEROSEXISM?

These are words you may have never heard before, but you may have felt them! **Heteronormativity** assumes that what is normal is being **heterosexual** (attracted to the opposite **gender**). This can be seen in TV shows, on forms people have to fill out, or even in the words people choose to use. (Remember, it is perfectly normal and healthy if you are not **heterosexual**.) **Heterosexism** is believing that **heterosexuals** are better than others, or that other orientations are wrong or less valuable. These are both biases that can make **LGBTQ+** individuals feel ignored, ashamed, and less important.

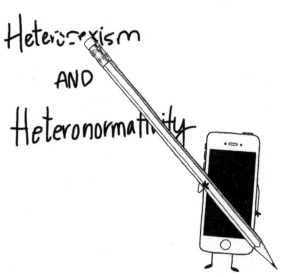

CHAPTER FIVE

"CAN YOU GET AN STI FROM A TOILET SEAT?"

AND OTHER QUESTIONS ABOUT SEXUALLY TRANSMITTED INFECTIONS

WHAT IS THE DIFFERENCE BETWEEN AN STI AND STD?

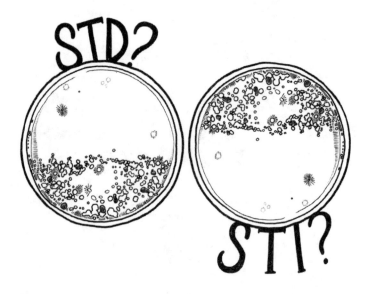

STI stands for **Sexually Transmitted Infection**. **STD** stands for **Sexually Transmitted Disease**. Even though they are different terms, they are talking about the exact same things. Many health care clinics and doctors have started using **STI** rather than **STD** because the bacteria or virus that was transmitted can create an infection, but that doesn't always turn into a *disease*, so "infection" better describes what they are.

I WOULD KNOW IF I HAVE AN STI, RIGHT?

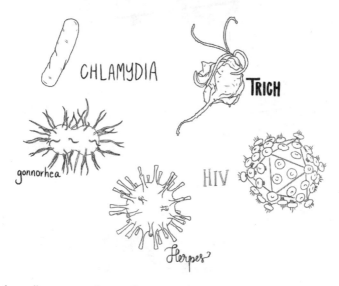

Actually, no, not always. Some common symptoms of **STIs** are discharge from the **penis** or **vagina**; sores/bumps/blisters on the **penis**, **vagina**, or anus; and pain or discomfort during **sex**. If any of these things are going on, you should see a **health care provider**. But, it is important to remember that many **STIs** show no symptoms! The only way to know for sure if a person has or does not have an **STI** is to go get tested.

*You have to ask for an **STI** test when you go to a **health care provider**. They don't just give one to you automatically.*

IS A COLD SORE HERPES?

Yes, a cold sore is a type of **herpes**. It is **herpes** simplex-1, and it is often found on the outside and inside of the mouth, and even in the nose. It is possible for **herpes** from the mouth to spread to the **penis**, **vagina**, or anus during **oral sex**. A person can get medicine for a **herpes** outbreak so that it is less painful and goes away faster. But even with medicine, **herpes** does not get "cured." That means the symptoms may come and go, but the **herpes** virus will live in the body forever. If someone has sores they can see or feel, its best to not have **sex**, because this is when people are more likely to pass it on.

LET'S SAY I MASTURBATE. IF I DO, CAN I GIVE MYSELF AN STI?

Masturbating is when someone touches their own sexual parts using their hands, a **sex** toy, or another object because it feels good. **Masturbation** is healthy and normal, and it is up to each person to decide whether it feels good to masturbate or not. Here is the good news: a person cannot give themselves an **STI**. If they already have an **STI**, they are not going to give it to themselves again. If they do not have an **STI**, they can't create one by masturbating.

Why Isn't **HIV** spread by HUGS, HANDSHAKES or KISSES?

HIV is a viral **Sexually Transmitted Infection (STI)**. That means if you get **HIV**, you will have it for the rest of your life. **HIV** is most commonly spread through specific bodily fluids: blood, **semen (cum)**, pre-ejaculate (**precum**), rectal fluids, **vaginal** fluids, and **breast** milk. Since most hugs, handshakes, and kisses do not usually share these fluids, **HIV** is not spread during these activities. FYI: you also cannot get **HIV** from sharing food, toilets, or drinks with a person with **HIV**.

HOW LONG DO YOU LIVE WHEN YOU GET HIV?

Just like any other infection, it is important to get treatment for **HIV**. If someone takes medicine to treat their **HIV**, they can live a long time. However, if someone doesn't receive treatment, the virus can progress into **AIDS**. **AIDS** stands for Acquired Immunodeficiency Syndrome, a condition that makes it so a person has a harder time fighting off infections. Developing **AIDS** could take anywhere from a few years to over 20 years.

CAN YOU GET AN STI LIKE... WITHOUT HAVING SEX WITH SOMEONE?

Most people get **STIs** from **oral**, **anal**, or **vaginal sex** with someone who already has an **STI**. There are a few other ways people can get an **STI** without having **sex**; one of these is through sexual skin-to-skin contact, which is how **herpes** is spread. People can also get some **STIs** from sharing needles, from **breast** milk, or during birth. So, yes, it is possible for someone who has not had **sex** to have an **STI**.

The most common **STI** is **HPV (Human Papilloma Virus)** which can be spread through sexual skin-to-skin contact. It is estimated that over 79 million Americans have **HPV**. Most of those people are in their teens and early 20s.[20]

No. If two people consent to having **sex** with each other and neither has an **STI**, they can't create an **STI** by having **sex** together. One person must have an **STI** to give it to another person. But it is possible that a person does not know they have an **STI**, and they can spread it to another person without knowing. Using a **condom** or **dental dam** can reduce the chance of spreading **STIs**. (Or your next date with each other can be getting tested together!)

*You can't tell if a person has an **STI** just by looking at them. Testing is the only way to know if you have one or not.*

VISIT
PLANNEDPARENTHOOD.org
FOR MORE INFO
-ICYC

CAN YOU GET AN STI FROM SITTING ON A TOILET SEAT?

If someone with an **STI** uses a toilet seat, it is not likely they will leave the fluids that **STIs** can live in on the seat. Fluids that STIs can live in include **vaginal** fluids, **semen, blood, breast milk, pre-cum,** and **rectal fluids. STIs** can't live long on a surface without these fluids. Suggestion: if you see these fluids on a toilet seat, maybe move on to the next stall. But let's say you don't and you sit down—you would need to have cuts on your thighs or butt that would make it easy for the bacteria or virus to enter your body in order to get the **STI**. So sit easy, because it's not likely.

An untreated **STI** is the most dangerous **STI**. The sooner someone gets tested and receives treatment, the better their health will be. Some **STIs**, long term, can cause **infertility** or even death if they go untreated, but with proper treatment people can live long, healthy lives. So go get tested!

WHAT WAS THE FIRST STI?

Just like other diseases, **STIs** have been around throughout history. Cloth **condoms** were documented as being used in ancient Egypt "to protect against disease."[21] Just like with many diseases, we do not know exactly when **STIs** started, but we do know how to prevent them from being passed from person to person, and we know how to diagnose them. Not having **sex** is the most effective way of preventing the spread of **STIs**. If someone is going to have **sex**, using an internal or external **condom** can help prevent getting an **STI**. And of course, getting tested regularly is a must!

WHAT'S THE *most* COMMON STI?

According to the CDC (Centers for Disease Control) the **Human Papilloma Virus** (**HPV**) is the most common **STI** in the United States. But the **STI** most reported to the CDC is **chlamydia**. It is important that if a person decides to be sexually active, they understand how to prevent getting and spreading **STIs**. Many people think "it won't happen to me" when it comes to **STIs**, but there would not be 24 million active cases of **HPV** in the United States if that were true. To learn more, visit texticyc.com.

IS A UTI AN STI?

UTI stands for **Urinary Tract Infection**. A **UTI** is not an **STI**. A person gets a **UTI** when bacteria gets into the **urethral** opening. It can cause a person to feel pain when they urinate, feel like they have to go to the bathroom all the time, or feel like even when they do pee, there is still a full **bladder**. If you think you have a **UTI**, it's important to get treated by a **health care provider**. If left untreated, UTIs can lead to more serious infections.

*Whenever someone has **sex**, it's a great idea to pee afterwards. This helps clean bacteria away from the **urethra** and helps prevent **UTIs**.*

It's not! **Yeast infections** are infections people can get without ever having **sex**. They are caused by the bacteria in the **vagina** getting out of balance. **Yeast infections** can come from using **antibiotics**, from not wearing breathable underwear, or from something else. However, their symptoms can be similar to some **STIs** (changes in discharge, itching, or pain with **vaginal sex**). A person who has these symptoms should talk to a **health care provider**. **Yeast infections** can also be passed to a partner or worsened by having **sex**, so it's important for a person to wait at least seven days after their symptoms go away and/or they have had treatment before having **sex** again.

Using **condoms** to help prevent **STIs** is a great idea. External **condoms** (**condoms** that go on the **penis**) and internal **condoms** (**condoms** that go inside the **vagina** or anus) work really well and create a barrier to prevent fluids from spreading from one partner to another. But some things to consider are: **condoms** are not 100% effective and they do not cover all of the skin in the **genital** area, so they do not always prevent *all* **STIs**. Even though **condoms** aren't 100% effective, they are still the most effective way to protect partners from the spreading of **STIs** during **sex**.

*If **condoms** aren't used correctly or aren't used during the entire sexual activity, there is still a risk of **pregnancy** and/or **STIs**. So if people start having **sex** and then put a **condom** on halfway through, they may not be protected.*

WHERE WOULD YOU BUY A DENTAL DAM IF FOR SOME REASON YOU REALLY WANTED ONE?

A **dental dam** is a thin piece of material, typically latex, that can be used during **oral sex** on the **vagina** or anus to prevent the spread of **STIs**. People can get a **dental dam** at local health centers or even purchase them online. If someone does not have a **dental dam**, they can cut open a latex **condom** to create a barrier.

...AND **THIS** IS A DENTAL DAM.

ARE THERE CONDOMS FOR WOMEN?

Yes! There are internal **condoms** made for **vaginas**. The **condom** is called FC2. The **condom** is inserted into the **vagina** and it can help prevent both **pregnancy** and **STIs**. (See the **Birth Control** chapter for steps on how to use an internal **condom**!)

Fun Facts About Internal **Condoms**:

▸ They can be inserted up to six hours ahead of time
▸ They're super lubricated
▸ They're made of nitrile, so they're great for a person who is allergic to latex
▸ Nitrile warms to body temperature, so people think it feels more natural
▸ They cover more of the vulva, which offers added protection from STIs spread through skin-to-skin contact

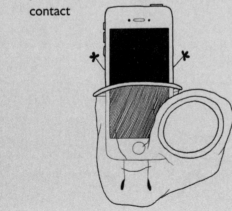

IS THERE ANY WAY TO PROTECT YOURSELF FROM STIS BEFORE HAVING SEX?

Absolutely! A person can get a vaccine to help prevent the most common strains of **HPV (Human Papilloma Virus)**. There is also a once-a-day pill called **PrEP (Pre-Exposure Prophylactics)** that can be taken to prevent **HIV**. Also, communicating with your partner about what type of protection to use and whether you've ever been tested can be a great way to help you stay safe!

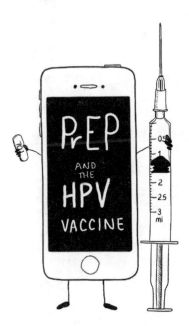

CAN YOU CURE AN STI?

Some **STIs** are curable and some are not. If the **STI** is bacterial (like **chlamydia**), it can be cured with **antibiotics**. If the **STI** is viral (like **herpes**), it cannot be cured. There are a variety of medications and treatments that can support a person in staying healthy if they live with a viral **STI**. The best way to know if a person has a viral or bacterial **STI** is to get tested.

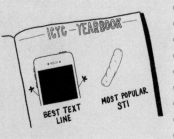

Chlamydia is the most common **STI** reported and is most common in young people. So, while you can get rid of **chlamydia** with proper treatment, you need to get tested to make sure you *can* treat it![22]

CAN I SHAVE MY PUBES TO GET RID OF CRABS?

"Pubes" is another word for **pubic hair**. Crabs are a parasite that grab onto **pubic hair**, lay eggs, and feed on blood by biting the skin (and yeah, under a microsope they actually look like little crabs). Crabs can be spread through sexual activity. Shaving **pubic hair** does not necessarily get rid of all crabs and eggs. It is important to use medicated shampoos on the infected area to make sure that all crabs and eggs have been removed. Talk to a trusted adult or **health care provider** for help.

HOW QUICKLY CAN YOU TELL IF YOU HAVE AN STI?

So many people want to go get tested the next day after having **sex**, but that won't tell you what you want to know. A person should typically wait two or three weeks after having **sex** before getting tested to make sure any **STIs** will show up on the test.[23] But don't wait too long to be tested because some people won't ever get symptoms. So, a person who is concerned that they might have an **STI** should go get tested whether they have symptoms or not. Remember, engaging in sexual activity without using **condoms** or **dental dams** increases your chance of getting an **STI**.

CAN I FIND OUT IF I HAVE AN STI BY PUTTING A LEMON ON MY PENIS?

Well, let's not do that, okay? Not only will it not tell a person if they have an **STI**, if lemon juice gets in the **urethra** it will *sting*. There are a lot of myths out there about how to tell if someone has an **STI**. Here is the truth: nothing will tell a person if they have an **STI** better than going to the doctor and getting tested. So put down that lemon and make an appointment!

SHOULD I WEAR GOGGLES TO AVOID GETTING CUM IN MY EYE?

Well, you could wear goggles, if you want to. But, it would be more effective to wear a **condom** on the **penis** or **sex toy** to avoid sharing fluids. It is possible to get an **STI** in the eyes and elsewhere anytime fluids are present in **oral**, **anal**, or **vaginal sex**.

ARE THERE ANY LIKE TONGUE CONDOMS FOR SEX?

Interesting, but no, it would be too much of a choking hazard. There is not a **condom** designed to be worn on the tongue, but there are **dental dams** (for **oral sex** on the **vagina** or anus) and external **condoms** (for **oral sex** on a **penis**) that someone can wear to protect themselves and their partner(s). If you are using an external **condom** on the **penis**, it might be a good idea to use a **condom** without spermicide on it. The spermicide is a chemical and does not taste good. Instead, you might want to try flavored **condoms**. Flavored **condoms** are specifically designed for **oral sex** on the **penis** and can be found at a drug store or health care center.

CAN YOU GET STIs ON YOUR HANDS... OR LIKE OTHER PLACES?

Wouldn't it be nice if the answer was no? But that is not always true. **STIs** such as **herpes**, **syphilis**, and **HPV** can be transmitted (shared) through skin-to-skin contact with an infected area. Even though it is possible to get infections on other parts of your body, the **genitals** and mouth are the most common parts to get infected. They don't call them **SEX**ually transmitted for nothing!

*Other ways **STIs** can pass are through blood, **semen**, **precum**/pre-ejaculate, **vaginal** or anal fluids, and **breast** milk.*

IS HPV WARTS OR CANCER?

HPV can be both… or more! **HPV** is a unique **STI** because it has lots of different strains (over 40!). This means there are a lot of different types of **HPV**. Some types of **HPV** can cause **genital warts**, which are cauliflower-shaped bumps that show up on the **genitals**. Other types of **HPV** don't cause bumps but can lead to different types of cancer if not treated. However, most types of **HPV** don't do anything noticeable, and symptoms often go away on their own. If a person has tested positive for **HPV**, it's important they talk to their doctor about the next steps when it comes to self care for the type of **HPV** they have.

WHAT'S THE BEST WAY TO KNOW IF MY PARTNER HAS AN STI?

You cannot tell if a person has an **STI** by the way they look, so the only way to know is to talk it out! Talking to your partner(s) about **STIs**, testing, and protection is important before deciding to be sexual together. If you're still concerned about potential **STIs**, go and get tested together. If someone won't get tested, you need to decide if that is a person you want to have a sexual relationship with. Because getting tested is super easy, and when it comes to being safe, you only have one body—so protect it!

HOW OFTEN SHOULD I GET TESTED?

How often a person should get tested depends on their sexual behavior. It is important to get tested with each new partner, or at least once a year. Even if someone has a long term partner, it's important to get tested at least once yearly. If someone is having **sex** with multiple partners, getting tested more often, like every three to six months, can help them and their partners stay informed about their health.

During annual check ups, not all doctors automatically test for **STIs**. *To make sure you are getting the tests you need, talk to your doctor about* **STI** *testing.*

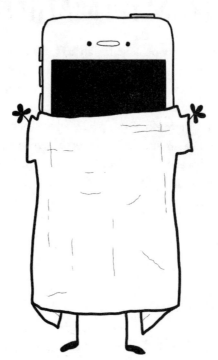

HOW SOON CAN YOU HAVE SEX AFTER STI TREATMENT?

When someone tests positive for an **STI**, they should wait at least seven days after finishing any medication prescribed and wait until their symptoms are gone before having sex again. Remember: some **STIs** are cured by medication whereas others are not. If someone has a viral **STI** (which cannot be cured) they need to use an internal or external **condom** to reduce the chance of spreading it to their partner. If you have recently had an **STI**, it's important to inform any new partners.

WHERE COULD I GO TO GET TESTED?

Great news—there are so many places a person can go to get tested! What's available to you depends on where you live. Doctor's offices, departments of health, and Planned Parenthood clinics all offer **STI** testing. Some schools also have clinics that can provide testing. To find a Planned Parenthood clinic near you, visit texticyc.com.

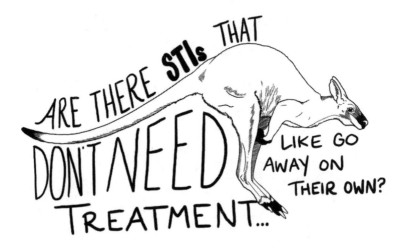

ARE THERE **STIs** THAT DON'T NEED TREATMENT... LIKE GO AWAY ON THEIR OWN?

Getting an **STI** is not like getting a cold, where you can just get some rest and eat some soup and it goes away. Almost no **STIs** go away on their own, even if their symptoms seem to. If you have an **STI**, it is important to go to a doctor to be treated. (After that, you can eat soup if you want. I get it. It's a comfort thing.) If **STIs** are left untreated, it is possible they can lead to more serious health problems.

*Certain strains of **HPV** can go away on their own. However, some other strands can cause cancer, so it is still important to get tested and treated!*

TODAY NEXT YEAR?

HPV RESULTS:

+ −

DO BUMPS DOWN THERE MEAN I HAVE AN STI?

Not always! It can be alarming to look down and see a random bump or rash on the **genitals**, but the truth is, that bump could be from a lot of different things. Yes, if you have had unprotected **oral**, **anal**, or **vaginal sex**, it could be a symptom of an **STI**, but it could also be something like an ingrown hair, allergic reaction, or even a pimple. The only way to know for sure is to get tested!

*Remember: some **STIs** like **herpes** and **HPV** can be passed just by naked **genital** skin-to-skin contact.*

How do I tell my NEW partner about my STI?

While this can feel uncomfortable, or even scary, it's a really important conversation to have. Before having **sex**, everyone deserves to know all the information they may need to make a decision about what's best for them. That includes ensuring your partner knows they have a chance of getting an **STI**. When you have the conversation, it can help to let them know you care about them and their health. You'll want to let them know what **STI** you have, how it's spread, and what you both can do to stay safe. Having an **STI** won't necessarily prevent you from having **sex**—you will just need to make sure you protect yourself and your partner with a **condom** or **dental dam** (which you should be doing anyway).

HOW DO I TELL SOMEONE THAT I MIGHT HAVE GIVEN THEM AN STI?

It might be as simple as a phone call or text. You would probably want to let them know that you were tested, that it came back positive, and you would recommend they get tested themselves. If talking in person, it can help to find a place that's private. Either way, thinking about what you want to say ahead of time can be helpful. This may feel hard, but it's important to be honest so people can get the testing and/or treatment they need. If this does not feel possible, you could use a service like https://dontspreadit.com/, where a person can anonymously inform people of their need to get tested.

CHAPTER SIX

"DO BABIES COME OUT OF THE BUTT?"

AND OTHER QUESTIONS ABOUT PREGNANCY

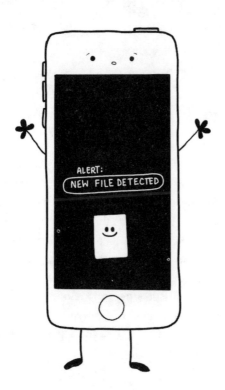

DO YOU HAVE TO DO YOU-KNOW-WHAT TO GET PREGNANT, OR CAN YOU GET PREGNANT JUST BY HANGING OUT WITH BOYS?

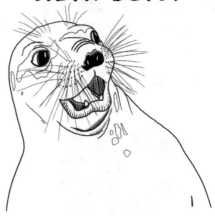

Pregnancy can only happen when **sperm** gets inside of a **vagina** and swims up to meet with an **egg** in the **uterus** (see page 288). This usually happens through, you guessed it, S-E-X. And even more specifically, through **vaginal sex**, when **semen** (which contains **sperm**) gets into a **vagina**. Sometimes people may also get pregnant without having **sex**, with the help of their doctor. But a person cannot get pregnant just by hanging out with someone. Can you imagine how many people would be pregnant if **pregnancy** could happen just through girls and boys hanging out together?

WHAT AGE CAN YOU GET PREGNANT?

A person with a **vagina** can get pregnant once they start to ovulate, or release **eggs**. This happens when a person starts going through **puberty**, just before they get their first **period**. Also, a person with a **penis** can cause a **pregnancy** as soon as they begin to make **sperm**, which happens during **puberty**. A person with a **vagina** can get pregnant any time between **puberty** (when they start releasing **eggs**) and **menopause** (when they stop releasing **eggs**). It's important to remember that sometimes our bodies may be ready for **pregnancy** before we are, so if you're planning on having **penis**-to-**vagina sex**, it's always a good idea to talk to your partner(s) about **birth control** options.

Nope! **Pregnancy** cannot happen from "mouth **sex**," more commonly known as **oral sex**. As mentioned before, **pregnancy** happens when **sperm** gets in the **vagina**. **Sperm** cannot get to the **vagina** from the mouth (even if that **sperm** goes down the throat of a person with a **vagina**). But, it is important to remember that people can get **STIs** from **oral sex**. Using a **condom** can help reduce the risk of **STIs**.

Most people believe this is not possible, but guess what, it is! Surprise! **Sperm** can live in the **uterus** for three to five days, which means that if **sperm** are present when the **egg** is released, it can become fertilized! Also, a person with a **vagina** can have blood leaving their body when it isn't their **period**. Some people with **vaginas** have **spotting** between their actual **periods**. If a person with a **vagina** is bleeding, for whatever reason, this doesn't mean they can't get pregnant if they have **penis**-to-**vagina sex**.

DOES IT REALLY HAPPEN THAT YOU COULD GET PREGNANT WHEN, OR EVEN THOUGH, A GUY PULLS OUT RIGHT AWAY?

Yeah, it really happens! Once the **penis** is erect (or hard), it releases pre-ejaculate (or **precum**) to lubricate the **urethra** inside the **penis**. A person can't control when that fluid releases. Pre-ejaculate can pick up **sperm** previously left over in the **urethra** on its way out of the body. Whenever there is **sperm**, there is the potential for a **pregnancy** if it is going into a **vagina**. Because of this, a **pregnancy** could occur even if the **penis** is pulled out before **ejaculation**.

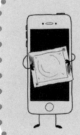

Pre-ejaculate or **precum** *can also contain any* **STIs** *a person might have. If you want to prevent* **pregnancy** *or* **STIs** *and still have sex, use a* **condom**.

CAN SOMEONE get pregnant WITH JUST ONE OVARY —OR— TESTICLE?

You better believe it! A person can still get pregnant or cause a **pregnancy** even if they only have one **ovary** or **testicle** (ball). Both **ovaries** have **eggs**, and each **testicle** makes **sperm**, so even if a person has only one, they are still releasing **eggs** or **sperm** from the one they have.

CAN YOU GET PREGNANT THE FIRST TIME YOU HAVE *sex?*

Yes, you can get pregnant the first time you have **sex**. **Sperm** and **eggs** do not care if it is the first time or the 50th time a person has had **sex** (in fact, they don't even know what number it is). Any time **sperm** gets into a **vagina**, a **pregnancy** can happen. If someone wants to have **sex** but reduce the chance of **pregnancy**, they should use **condoms** and/or **birth control** to reduce risk.

HOW DO I KNOW IF I AM PREGNANT?

You'll definitely know if you have a baby, but the best way to find out if you're pregnant earlier than that is to take a **pregnancy** test. However, you can't take a test right after **sex**. Tests work as soon as two weeks after **sex**, or one week after a missed **period**. Some of the most common signs of **pregnancy** are missing a **period**, swollen or tender **breasts**, and nausea; but taking a test is the only way to know for sure.[24]

HOW DOES PEEING ON A PREGNANCY STICK TELL YOU IF YOU'RE PREGNANT OR NOT?

So, it's not a stick from a tree, but a special tool that measures **hormones** that are only present in pee (or urine) when a person is pregnant. The **hormone** is called hCG. If the **hormone** is in the body, the test will show a positive result. If a person buys a **pregnancy** test at the store, they need to read the directions to make sure they are using the test correctly, since each test is different. A person can also go into a doctor or clinic to get a **pregnancy** test.

IF I GET PREGNANT, HOW DO I KNOW WHAT OPTION IS RIGHT FOR ME?

PARENTING

ABORTION

ADOPTION

When someone finds out they are pregnant, they have three choices they can make. First, they can continue their **pregnancy** and choose to parent. Second, they can continue their **pregnancy** and choose adoption. Finally, they can end their **pregnancy** by choosing **abortion**. For some people this is an easy decision, and for others this can be a difficult decision. It is important to know all your options, talk to people in your life who are important to you, understand how each option will affect you, and make the decision that is best for you. For more resources about pregnancy options, see page 265.

Some things to think about when making this decision are:
- *Future Goals*
- *Finances*
- *State Laws*
- *Supportive people in your life*
- *Personal values*

Is abortion Okay? How's it done?

People have many different opinions about **abortion**. Some people think it is okay, and some don't. Talking with someone you trust about how you feel about **abortion** can be helpful when trying to decide what is right for you. **Abortions** can be done safely by getting a prescription for medication to end the **pregnancy** at home, or by having a doctor end the **pregnancy** at a clinic. If you choose **abortion**, talking with your doctor can help you decide which method is best for you.

WILL HAVING AN ABORTION AFFECT MY CHANCES OF GETTING PREGNANT IN THE FUTURE?

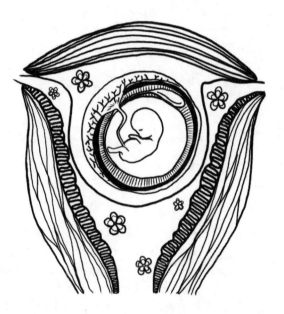

Having an **abortion** is not likely to change your chances of getting pregnant in the future. There is no evidence that an **in-clinic** or **medication abortion** will affect someone's ability to get pregnant. **Abortion** does not affect the **ovaries** or the **eggs**.

I HAVE HEARD ABOUT OPEN AND CLOSED ADOPTION, WHAT IS THE DIFFERENCE?

Open adoptions often refer to there being continued contact, or the option for contact, between the birth parent(s) and the adoptive family and child. This could mean anything from yearly updates through pictures to actual visits between the birth parent(s) and adoptive family. In a closed adoption, the birth parent(s) agrees, typically before birth, to not have any contact with the adoptive family and child.

WHAT HAPPENS TO THE BODY DURING PREGNANCY?

So much! The **uterus** expands, the **breasts** may swell as they get ready to make milk, the person may go through hormonal and emotional changes, the body can gain weight, and even the feet can get bigger, just to name a few. When a person gets pregnant, their body starts working to grow a **fetus**. A full-term **pregnancy** usually lasts nine months, which is time for a lot of changes. **Pregnancy** is a unique experience for everyone who goes through it.

Book after book has been written on this subject alone. Check out the Wrap Up *for some recommendations.*

DO BABIES COME OUT OF THE BUTT?

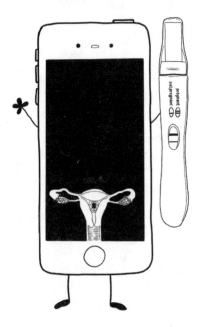

The answer is a big no, babies do not come out of the butt. If a person has a **vaginal** birth, the baby is pushed out of the **uterus**, through the **cervix**, and out of the **vagina**. Some people have a **C-section** (cesarean section), which is a surgery. This surgery is performed in a hospital and involves the doctor cutting into the **uterus** through the skin to remove the baby.

I HEARD PEOPLE TALKING ABOUT A MISCARRIAGE, WHAT IS IT?

A **miscarriage** is when a **pregnancy** ends unexpectedly. Most **miscarriages** happen in the first few months of **pregnancy**. It can happen for many reasons, often because the **fetus** is not developing normally. It is typical for the person to not know why it happened. **Miscarriages** are actually really common,[25] but most people don't know that because people don't always talk about **miscarriages** or their experiences with them.

CAN YOU HAVE SEX WHEN YOU'RE PREGNANT?

As long as your doctor hasn't given you other instructions, **sex** is safe during **pregnancy**. It will not hurt the baby because the baby is inside the **uterus**. If the person is having **vaginal sex**, the **penis** stays in the **vagina** and cannot go into the **uterus**. Other forms of **sex** are also safe during **pregnancy**.

WHY CAN PREGNANCY BE PAINFUL WHEN THE BABY COMES OUT?

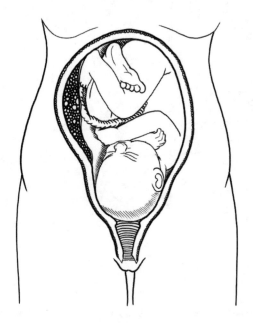

Giving birth is painful for a few reasons. The **uterus** is contracting (squeezing) to push the baby out (think about **period** cramps but much more intense). The **cervix**, which is really sensitive and small, is opening and being stretched. The **vagina** and the **vaginal** opening are also stretching to allow for a baby to pass through. All of this squeezing and stretching can be very uncomfortable, or even very painful. How painful and uncomfortable depends on the person, the size of the baby, and if they are using any pain medication.

If a person's pushing really hard while having a baby, it's definitely possible they might pee. Some people even poop when they are giving birth. The muscles used to poop are the same muscles used to push a baby out. Peeing or pooping during childbirth is totally normal.

WHY DO PEOPLE BREATHE FUNNY DURING LABOR?

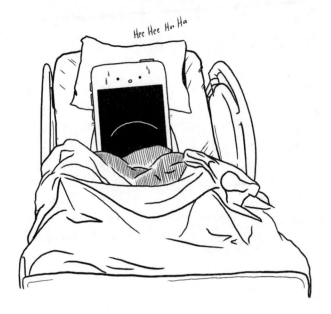

It does sound kind of funny—most people don't breathe like that when they are sitting in class or doing errands. This type of breathing is called patterned breathing, and many people learn how to do it because it can help make **labor** a little easier to go through. The patterned breathing can help the person concentrate, can increase oxygen in the bloodstream, and can be calming during **labor**.[26]

AFTER BIRTH, IS YOUR VAGINA STILL THE SAME? OR DOES THE VAGINA GO BACK TO NORMAL SIZE?

Well, not immediately, but the **vagina** is a muscle and is made to stretch. During **pregnancy** and birth, the release of **hormones** allows for the **vagina** to open and change shape. If someone has a **vaginal** birth (the baby comes out of the **vagina**), the **vagina** is going to change and expand during the birth. But typically, over time the **vagina** will return to a size and shape that's similar to how it was prior to birth. After the recommended "nothing in the **vagina** for the first six weeks" **period**, sexual partner(s) shouldn't notice much of a difference at all.[27]

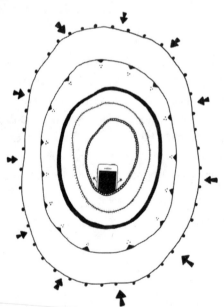

IF SOMEONE CUMS (IN A POOL) WILL EVERYONE GET PREGNANT?

First, a person should not ejaculate into a pool because that isn't a private place and the people swimming have not given consent, nor do they want to be exposed to ejaculate when they are swimming. **Pregnancy** can only happen if **sperm** enters the **uterus** and meets an **egg**. So, if two people are having **sex** in a pool, **pregnancy** can totally happen, but only between the two of them. If someone is ejaculating on their own into a pool, the chemicals, distance, and all that water is going to make **pregnancy** nearly impossible.[28]

IF A LIL' PIECE OF CUM GETS IN YOU, CAN IT GET YOU PREGNANT?

It only takes one **sperm** to fertilize an **egg** and cause a **pregnancy**. **Semen** (**cum**) is the fluid that **sperm** live in. Even if a person only releases a little bit of **semen** (or pulls the **penis** out just as they are ejaculating), it is possible that **pregnancy** could happen. Most people release from half a teaspoon to a full teaspoon of **semen** each time they ejaculate.

*In a teaspoon of **semen** there are hundreds of millions of **sperm**.*[29] *In fact, the average **ejaculation** has 200 million **sperm**!*

CAN YOU GET PREGNANT WHEN YOU DO IT DOGGYSTYLE?

You absolutely can get pregnant from doggystyle. This is a slang term for a sexual position. When talking about **vaginal sex**, no matter the position or its name, there is a risk of **pregnancy**. If **sperm** gets into the **vagina**, a **pregnancy** may happen; **condoms** and other forms of **birth control** are a great way to prevent this. There are so many different ways to have sex—it's important to talk to your partner about what you do or don't want.

HOW ARE TWINS MADE?

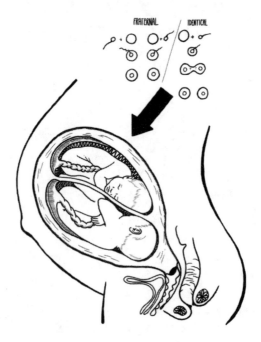

Some people want to know how twins are made because they want twins, and some people want to know so they *never* have twins. But a person doesn't have control over whether they have twins. Twins happen in two ways (ha! "Two ways."). Identical twins—twins that have the exact same genetic make-up and look exactly alike—happen when one **egg** is released and one **sperm** enters that **egg**. The fertilized **egg** then splits in half and creates two babies. Fraternal twins—twins that may look similar, but not exactly the same—happen when two **eggs** are released, and one **sperm** enters one **egg** while a different **sperm** enters the other **egg**.

HOW MANY CHILDREN COULD SOMEONE HAVE AT ONCE?

There have been two women who have had eight babies at one time. Both of the women had help from doctors in getting pregnant. When it comes to that many babies at once, it can't happen without the help of a doctor. But twins, triplets, and even quadruplets can happen naturally, without a doctor's help. It is important that a pregnant person gets prenatal care (health care while the baby is growing); a person with multiple babies often needs to be seen by a doctor more often to make sure that they and babies are healthy.

Morning sickness, or throwing up, is really common during the **first trimester** (twelve weeks) of **pregnancy**, but can last the whole **pregnancy**. No one knows exactly why it happens, but there are some ideas. For example, it could be from the increased amount of **hormones** during **pregnancy**, or it could be from reduced blood sugar. The other thing to know is that **morning sickness** doesn't just happen in the morning. Some people have it all day, at night, or not at all.[30]

CAN I MISS A PERIOD WITHOUT BEING PREGNANT?

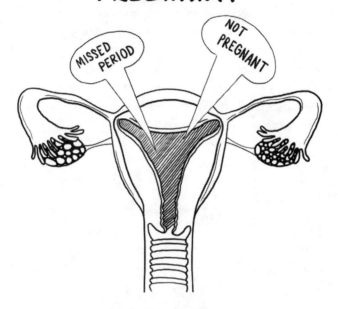

I'm late! For a very important date! Wait . . . am I? A lot of people worry about **pregnancy** if they miss a **period**, or if their **period** comes later than expected, but there are a lot of different reasons why this may happen! Sometimes stress, exercise, or diet can impact a person's **period**. And for teens, **periods** can be irregular anyways! If you're ever worried about being pregnant, take a **pregnancy** test.

CAN YOU GET PREGNANT FROM PRECUM?

It is possible to get pregnant from **precum**. **Precum** is the flu-id that leaves the **penis** before a person ejaculates (**cums**). A person cannot control or feel when **precum** leaves the body. While most **precum** does not have **sperm** in it, or has dead **sperm** in it, small amounts of live **sperm** can be released or picked up as **precum** leaves the body. So while the chances are small, it is possible. Using **condoms** the entire time a person has **sex** is a great way to protect against **pregnancy**.[31]

DON'T YOU need a period BEFORE you can get PREGNANT?

A lot of people think this! There is actually a small chance a person can get pregnant before their first **period**. This is because they may have their first **ovulation** (release of an **egg**) in the few weeks before their first **period**. If the person has unprotected **vaginal sex** during this time, it is possible they could get pregnant.

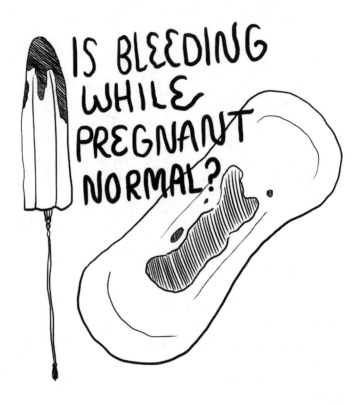

It's possible to have some **spotting** or light bleeding when pregnant, but it's not common (and it's not a **period**). If someone is having any bleeding while they're pregnant, it's important they talk to their doctor immediately to make sure they and their **pregnancy** are healthy.

can you still have a

baby

if you have an STI?

The easy answer is yes. All **STIs** can be treated, and as long as they are treated right away, it shouldn't change whether or not a person can get pregnant or cause a **pregnancy**. If an **STI** is left untreated, it can get worse and cause damage that may make it harder for a **pregnancy** to happen. If someone has an **STI** and they are pregnant, it is possible to pass it to the baby (**fetus**) during **pregnancy**, birth, or **breast** feeding. Anytime someone thinks they have an **STI** it is important to get tested and talk with a **health care provider**.

CHAPTER SEVEN

"WAIT, CONDOMS EXPIRE?"

AND OTHER QUESTIONS ABOUT BIRTH CONTROL

I HAD SEX ALREADY, CAN I STILL BE ABSTINENT?

Absolutely! **Abstinence** means that someone is not having **sex**. Anybody can choose not to have **sex** at any time in their life—even if they have had **sex** before. **Abstinence** is the most effective method of protection against **pregnancy** and **sexually transmitted infections**. You get to decide what's best for you in terms of when or whether you are abstinent.

The honest answer is, the best **birth control** is the **birth control** that you will use! Everyone is different, so the method that works best for each person will be different, too. Some methods are more effective than others when used the correct way, so choosing one you'll use the right way every time is important.

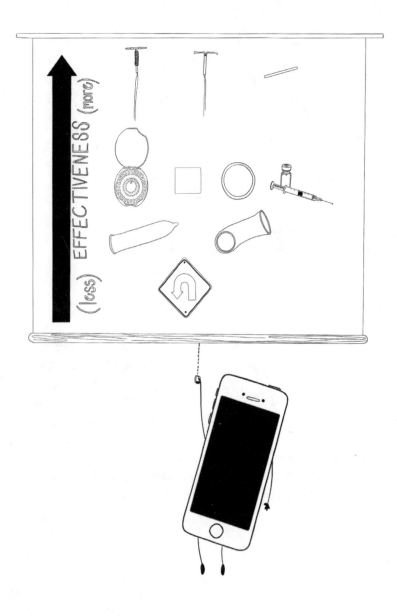

WHY DO CONDOMS HAVE TO BE PUT ON A CERTAIN WAY?

Condoms are most effective when used correctly. The steps to putting on a **condom** ensure that the **condom** works.

Make sure the **condom** hasn't expired and there is no visible damage to the wrapper.

Slide the **condom** to the side of the package and tear along the ridges of the wrapper to open. It's important to use your hands to open the **condom** and not the cool samurai sword hanging above your bed.

Don't just jump to putting the **condom** on the **penis**. Make sure it's right side up by checking that it is the right direction on your finger. If the **condom** is right side up, it will easily unroll. If it doesn't unroll, flip it over before putting it on the **penis**.

Pinch the tip of the **condom**. This makes it so no extra air is trapped in the **condom**. This is no time for a balloon animal. Blocking off this space also allows room for fluids that will be released by the **penis** during **sex**.

Roll the **condom** down the length of the **penis**. Not halfway, *all the way*. This also needs to happen *after* someone has an **erection** to make sure the **condom** fits.

Holding the base of the **condom** makes sure it doesn't slip off when **pulling out**. Often after **ejaculation** a person can start to lose their **erection**. Without an **erection**, the **condom** may not fit properly.

It's never a bad idea to tie a knot in the **condom** so the fluid doesn't escape. **Condoms** go in the trash, not the toilet or the sink, and are never reused.

An internal **condom** is a condom option that is inserted into the **vagina** or **anus**. Just like with external **condoms**, it's important to check the package and open carefully. Once the **condom** is out, make sure there is a ring inside of the **condom** and that you don't see any tears. Pinch the internal ring inside the **condom** and insert it into the **vagina**. The larger ring should remain on the outside of the body. Once finished with the **condom**, twist the outside ring and pull the **condom** out. Throw the **condom** away in the trash.

Are **2** condoms better than **1**?

Ask Your Questions by TEXTING "ICYC?" to 57890

Actually, no! People don't wear two bike helmets at once, do they? Two **condoms** will not make someone safer. **Condoms** are designed to be worn one at a time. If someone insists on using two **condoms**, it is important to add lubrication between each **condom** to reduce friction. If there is friction, it increases the chance of each **condom** breaking.

HOW DO I EVEN GET BIRTH CONTROL?

There are lots of different ways to get **birth control**. **Condoms** can be bought online or at most gas stations, pharmacies, and grocery stores, and other methods can be prescribed at a clinic or doctor's office. Before someone chooses to use any **birth control** method, it's important they know how to use it properly. Thinking about how well they want it to work, how much it will cost, and how using the method will fit into their lifestyle can help a person decide what the best fit is for them.

HOW OLD DO I HAVE TO BE TO GET BIRTH CONTROL?

Depending on where you live, there might be different laws around **birth control** (check out the Wrap-Up for resources on **birth trol**). In some places, there aren't any age limits for **birth control**. In other places, people may need to be a certain age, have parental permission, or meet other state requirements before getting a prescription.

*There is no age restriction for **condoms**!*

PATIENT NAME: _____

DOB: _____

Prescription:

Why do I have to go to the doctor for the pill but not condoms?

Signature: _____ Date: _____

Lucky you—you actually can get **condoms** at the doctor's office, too! Even though the pill is generally very safe, it and other hormonal methods of **birth control** require a doctor's visit and prescription. It's important that a medical professional works with you to make sure the **birth control** is a good fit for you and is safe. Just like any other medication, hormonal **birth control** can have side effects (headaches, changes in mood, and nausea). It's important to talk openly and honestly with your doctor about any existing health conditions to make sure they find the best method for your body and its unique needs. On the other hand, **condoms** don't usually have any side effects unless someone is allergic to the material, so you can get them at the store or even online.

Things to consider when choosing a birth control method:

▸ *Cost*
▸ *Whether it contains hormones, and how much*
▸ *How well it works*
▸ *How and when it's used*
▸ *Who it's used by*
▸ *STI protections*

Co$t varie$ depending on the **birth control** method and where a per$on i$ getting their method. **Condom$** are often given out at health center$ for free, or can be bought in pack$ for only a few dollar$. People can u$e in$urance and Medicaid to help pay, or fully pay, for their pre$cription **birth control** method$. If a per$on is worried about the co$t of their cho$en **birth control**, $ome place$ offer a$$i$tance. It can al$o be helpful to talk to a tru$ted adult.

WHY WOULD YOU TAKE *birth control* IF YOU'RE NOT HAVING SEX?

Birth control is used for lots of reasons beyond **pregnancy** prevention. Some hormonal **birth control** methods can help clear up acne, reduce **period** cramps, lighten **periods**, make **periods** more regular, or take away **periods** all together. Just because someone is taking **birth control**, it doesn't mean they are having **sex**.

CAN I STILL HAVE BABIES IN THE FUTURE IF I TAKE BIRTH CONTROL?

Any reversible **birth control** method isn't going to change how likely someone is to get pregnant when they aren't using the method. **Birth control** only works when you are using it correctly and consistently; this means taking your pill every day, getting your shot on time, or using a **condom** every time you have **sex**. If someone is deciding to get off a prescribed **birth control** method, it's important they talk to their doctor.[32]

There are also some forms of **birth control** that are permanent, called **vasectomy** and **tubal ligation** (sometimes called **sterilization**), which are surgeries that block the **egg** or **sperm** from being able to meet.

CAN PEOPLE TAKE ALL THE HORMONE TYPES AT THE SAME TIME? WOULD IT WORK BETTER?

It's totally unnecessary to take more than one hormonal method of **birth control** at the same time unless prescribed by your doctor. It doesn't make it work any better. In fact, if you're using one method and using it the right way, it works really well! Taking a higher dose could cause even more side effects. Even though you can't use more than one hormonal method at a time unless a doctor says to, you can use **condoms** with any other **birth control** method. **Condoms** can help prevent not only **pregnancy**, but **STIs** too.

You can have your cake and **birth control,** too! Most people don't gain weight when they get on **birth control.**[33] Hormonal methods can have many different side effects, and one side effect can be weight gain. However, most of the time weight gain isn't from the birth control itself, but from your habits or from natural changes to your body as you grow up. The great thing is there are many types of **birth control** to choose from, so if the side effects of one aren't working for you, you can talk to your doctor about another kind!

THE CONDOM MADE MY VAGINA BURN. WHAT HAPPENED?

No need to call the fire department—latex allergies are very common! When someone has an allergy to latex, symptoms can include burning, itching, and pain. Most **condoms** are made of latex, but if a person is allergic they can use *non-latex* **condoms**. Most non-latex **condoms** are made of a material called polyisoprene, and they work the same way as latex **condoms** to protect against **pregnancy** and **STIs**.

*There are also lambskin **condoms**, but these only protect against **pregnancy**, not **STIs**.*

There are so many different types of **condoms**. Some have **lubricants** that heat up, some have ridges, and others come in colors. What really matters is what the condom is made out of. In order to prevent a pregnancy, it needs to be made out of latex, polyurethane, polyisoprene, or lambskin (though lambskin doesn't protect against STIs). Since most external **condoms** have the same level of effectiveness, the "best" **condom** is the **condom** that feels the best to you. Finding a **condom** that works well for you and your partner may take trying a few different kinds. Once you find a brand you like, storing it correctly will make sure it continues to work for you every time.

*How to store your **condoms**:*

▶ *At room temperature (cozy is best!)*
▶ *Out of direct sunlight (sunlight is too hot)*
▶ *Not in a car (in a car is extra hot)*
▶ *Not in a freezer (a freezer is too cold)*
▶ *Not in your wallet (too much rubbing)*

WHAT IF THE CONDOM BROKE?

Wow, that can be scary! Whether the **condom** broke, a partner didn't pull out, or a person didn't take their **birth control** correctly, **Emergency Contraception** (EC) can be used by a person with a **vagina** up to three to five days after having unprotected **vaginal sex** to prevent **pregnancy**. **Emergency Contraception** does not help with the prevention of **STIs**, so if the **condom** broke and you are concerned about **STIs**, you should get tested. See the following question for more information on **emergency contraception**.

CAN ANYONE BUY EMERGENCY CONTRACEPTION?

ICYC **loves** partner responsibility for protection! **Emergency Contraception** (or EC) is an **over-the-counter birth control** method that can be purchased at pharmacies. It may be on the shelf, kept behind the counter, or kept in a locked case, but no prescription is required. EC is meant to be used by someone with a **vagina** after unprotected **sex**. Because EC can be bought without a prescription, their partner can go into the store and get it for them. If someone wants to use their insurance, they would need to get a prescription themselves.

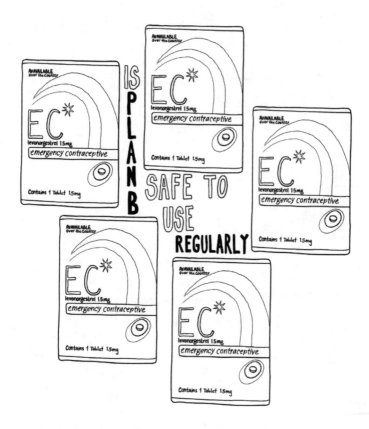

Emergency Contraception, like **Plan B**, is safe and can be used whenever someone needs it! It won't hurt someone if they use it often, but it's not meant to be anyone's go-to method of **birth control** for a few reasons: it doesn't work as well as other forms of **birth control**, it can get expensive, and it can have some annoying side effects. So if looking for a regular method of **birth control**, there are many other types that are more effective (and cost effective!). Remember, EC is the only form of **birth control** a person with a **vagina** can use after they have already had **sex**![34]

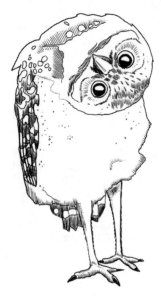

IS EMERGENCY CONTRACEPTION AN ABORTION?

Sometimes people get EC and **abortion** confused because they don't realize how they are different. **Abortion** is the safe ending of a **pregnancy**, while EC works to *prevent* a **pregnancy** from happening. EC is not **abortion**. It works to protect against **pregnancy** by stopping the **ovary** from releasing an **egg**, and if the **egg** has already been released, it thickens **cervical mucus** to block the **egg** and **sperm** from meeting. If **pregnancy** has already happened, it won't do anything.

Nothing is for everyone, except maybe pizza. A lot goes into the choice to use or not use **birth control**. Cost, effectiveness, side effects, or values can all influence a person's choice. Some people may choose to never use **birth control**, and that's A-OK! As long as a person feels in control of their choice, it's the right choice for them. (Also, not every type of **birth control** can be used by every body, so if you do choose to use **birth control**, make sure to choose the method that is right for your body.)

Values can come from a person's religious identity, community, education, family, personal experiences, and so many other influences!

HOW DO I KNOW IF I SHOULD BE USING A MAGNUM [CONDOM]?

While "magnum" really is an awesome name for a **condom**, regular-size **condoms** fit most people, fitting snugly on the **penis**. If a **condom** is hurting, or if they keep breaking, you may want to try a larger size (like a magnum). Similarly, if **condoms** keep slipping off, you may want to try a smaller size. For the best protection, do not use a size that is too large (or too small) for you. Make sure you are using the **condom** you and your body need.

WHAT ARE MY OPTIONS IF I ALWAYS FORGET TO TAKE THE PILL?

It can be hard to remember to take a **pill** every day, even with an alarm going off to remind you in the middle of breakfast! Great news: there are so many other healthy and effective **birth control** options that a person doesn't have to think about daily (like the patch, ring, or shot). If a person wants their method to work for 3-12 years without changing it, they can use a LARC (long-acting reversible **contraception**) like an **IUD** or **implant**.

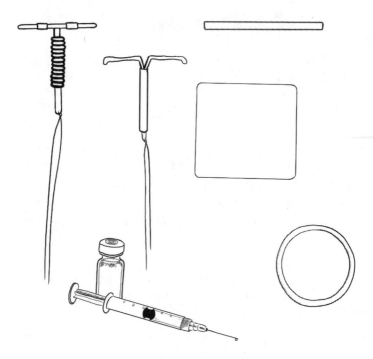

ISN'T BIRTH CONTROL KIND OF THE GIRL'S RESPONSIBILITY?

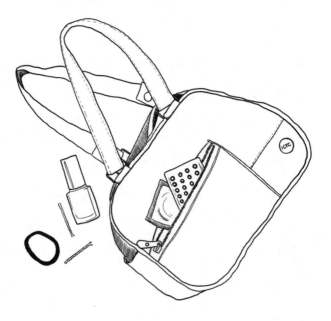

Birth control and **STI** protection is the responsibility of everyone who is having **sex**, not just one partner. Communicating with your partner about protection is a healthy way to share the responsibility. Even if only one person is using the protection method, both partners should be informed about how it works and what it requires. There are birth control options for all types of bodies, which means that any partner of any gender can use protection. Some partners even choose to share the cost!

CAN YOU USE A BALLOON, TRASH BAG, PLASTIC BAG, SANDWICH BAG, ETC. AS A CONDOM?

No matter what you've seen on TV or in a movie, it is not safe to use anything besides a **condom** as a **condom**. Balloons, trash bags, sandwich bags, etc., aren't made for **sex**. This means they may not be safe or clean for the body, and they won't protect against **pregnancy** or **STIs**. Using latex, polyurethane, or polyisoprene **condoms** that fit well and are not expired can help prevent **pregnancy** and **STIs**. If you can't afford **condoms**, many clinics give them away for free!

HOW DOES A COPPER IUD WORK? COULD YOU USE A PENNY INSTEAD?

First things first—*do not use a penny as* **birth control**. Gross! Here is some good news: the copper **IUD** is one of the most effective **birth control** methods. It works in a few ways. One is that copper is toxic to sperm, making them unable to swim to meet an **egg**. Another is that the copper makes the mucus in the **uterus** thicker. Both of these prevent the sperm from being able to reach the **egg**.

WHAT ARE FLAVORED CONDOMS FOR?

Condoms can help reduce the spread of **STIs**, but let's be real—latex doesn't taste great. So some people may choose to use **condoms** with flavoring on them when they have **oral sex** (in this case, mouth-to-**penis sex**). Never use flavored **condoms** during **vaginal** or **anal sex** because it can cause irritation.

IS THERE ANY WAY TO SKIP MY PERIOD

Yep! Sure is! Hormonal **birth control** methods can help reduce the amount of blood and the length of someone's **period**. In fact, there are some methods, like the **implant** and hormonal **IUD**, that can even stop **periods** altogether in some people. And yes, it's totally safe. If this is something you are interested in, you should definitely talk to a **health care provider** first. They can talk you through how to change up your current method, or help you find a new one, as well as talk you through any possible side effects.

I HEARD YOU CAN JUST TAKE YOUR TEMPERATURE INSTEAD OF USING BIRTH CONTROL, IS THAT TRUE?

Well, there is quite a bit more to it than just taking your temperature to prevent **pregnancy**. The idea is that when a person's body is getting ready to release an **egg**, or ovulate, their temperature changes. Taking your temperature is only one part of a **birth control** method called the "**Fertility** Awareness Method." **Fertility** awareness method is also sometimes called natural **family planning**, calendar method, rhythm method, or basal body temperature method. The person is monitoring their **menstrual cycle** (when they have a **period**, when they release an **egg**), body temperature, and even **hormone** levels to figure out when they are most likely

to be fertile; by do-ing so, the person can know when they should avoid **sex** so they don't get pregnant. This method can be effective, but it takes a lot of practice and getting to know your body really well![35]

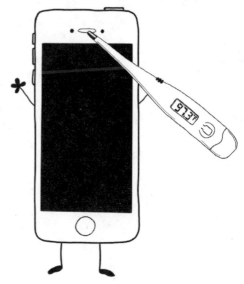

WAIT, CONDOMS EXPIRE?

Yep, just like milk expires, so do **condoms**. All **condoms** have an expiration date on them. It is important to use them before they expire. Once they expire, they do not curdle like milk, but they can break easier. If you are about to have **sex** and you notice the **condom** is expired, the best thing to do is to stop what you're doing and get another **condom**. If you don't have another **condom**, you can keep making out and just stop before **sex** happens, or you can stop altogether and do something else—like drink a glass of milk!

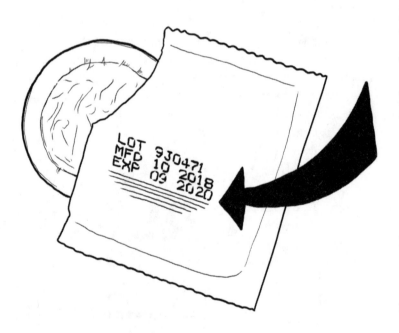

do gay people still need to use protection?

It doesn't matter what **gender identity** or **sexual orientation** someone is—it's always important to talk about protection with all sexual partners. Protection can look different for different relationships. Even if people are not worried about **pregnancy**, using **condoms** or **dental dams** can help reduce the risk of **STIs**. Getting tested for **STIs** regularly and/or between partners can also help keep people protected.

IS THERE BC FOR MEN?

Yep, there sure are **birth control** options for people with **penises**. First: the most effective option is **abstinence**, or not having **sex**. If someone wants to have **sex** and still be protected, they can use an external **condom**. Another **birth control** option for people with **penises** is the **withdrawal** method (**pull-out method**), although this is less effective than **condoms** in preventing **pregnancy**, and does not necessarily prevent **STIs**. Another option, to prevent **pregnancy** but not **STIs**, is a surgery called a **vasectomy**. A **vasectomy** is a permanent form of **birth control**, and may not be available to people under a certain age. There is currently research happening to provide more options to prevent **pregnancy**; so new methods might be coming soon. Even though a person with a **penis** can't take **the pill** or the patch, they can still help their partner with **birth control** reminders or by sharing the cost.

CAN I USE A TAMPON WITH AN IUD?

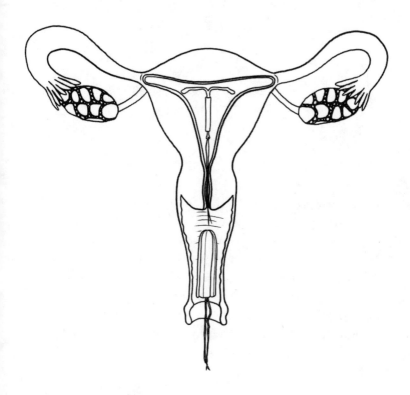

Totally! Lots of people use **tampons** when they have an **IUD**. **Tampons** are put in the **vagina**, whereas **IUDs** go in the **uterus**—two totally different places! Even though the strings of the **IUD** hang into the **vagina**, it shouldn't cause any problems if a person uses a **tampon**.

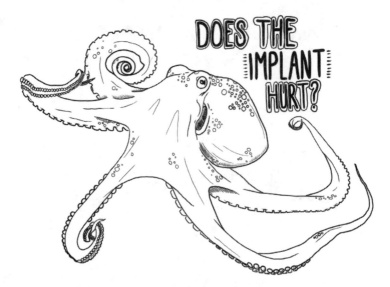

DOES THE IMPLANT HURT?

It shouldn't! Before the **birth control implant** is inserted into the arm, the doctor or nurse will make an injection that numbs the area where the **implant** will go. Some people may find this injection a little uncomfortable, but the actual insertion of the **implant** shouldn't hurt. After it's in place, people may notice some bruising and soreness on their arm for the next couple days. If the arm becomes very painful or a person is having trouble doing their normal activities, they should go back to their doctor immediately.

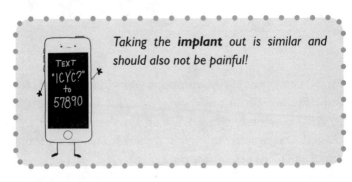

TEXT "ICYC?" to 57890

*Taking the **implant** out is similar and should also not be painful!*

That depends, are you talking five minutes late or five days late? **The pill** works best when used the right way, every single time, and that means taking it around the same time every single day. If someone takes their **birth control** later than usual (like in the same day, but later in the day), its effectiveness (how well it prevents **pregnancy**) may go down. And if a **pill** is actually missed, a person should check in with their doctor. If worried, use a backup method like a **condom** until back on schedule.

DOES THE PULL OUT method ACTUALLY WORK?

The pull-out method is also called the **withdrawal** method. It is when a person pulls the **penis** out before ejaculting. When used the right way every time, it can lower the chances of **pregnancy**. In order to use it the right way, a person needs to know their body really well, and this can take practice. Using a backup method like **condoms** until someone is confident in their ability to pull out will offer added protection.

No, **condoms** are a one-time use only! Using a **condom** again makes it more likely to break, and there is no way to make sure all the **sperm**, bacteria, or viruses are gone after you've washed it out. **Condoms** have only been proven to work when used one time. Don't do it—get a new **condom** for each act of **sex**.

CAN YOU USE CONDOMS IN THE SHOWER... OR THE OCEAN?

Condoms can be used in water. The important thing to make sure of if having **sex** in water is that the **condom** stays on. It's possible the force of the water in the shower or the ocean could cause the **condom** to slip off. Water can also wash away natural or water-based **lube**, so choosing a silicone **lube** can be more comfortable. Bacteria from the ocean could also get in the **vagina/penis** and cause irritation or infection. So while it's possible, that's a lot of things to think about compared to **sex** on land!

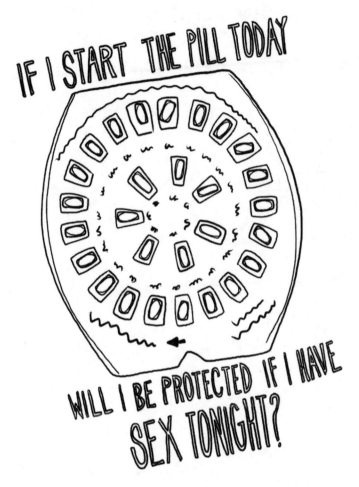

IF I START THE PILL TODAY WILL I BE PROTECTED IF I HAVE SEX TONIGHT?

Not so fast. **Birth control pills** usually take up to seven days to start protecting against **pregnancy**, unless your doctor tells you otherwise. Using a backup method like **condoms** for the first seven days will help protect against **pregnancy** while the body adjusts to **the pills**. Using **condoms** even after **the pills** have started working can continue to protect against **STIs**.

HOW DO I ASK MY PARTNER TO USE A CONDOM?

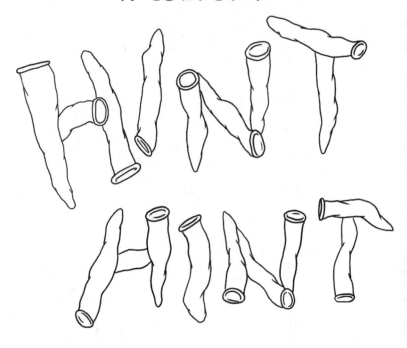

It can be as easy as, "Hey, let's use a **condom**," "What protection should we use?" or even, "I don't want to keep going unless we use a **condom**." Talking about protection is really important, but it doesn't have to be awkward. Speaking up for what you do or don't want in any sexual experience will help you feel more comfortable and protected.

CHAPTER EIGHT

"WHY DO BROKEN HEARTS HURT SO BADLY?"

AND OTHER QUESTIONS ABOUT RELATIONSHIPS

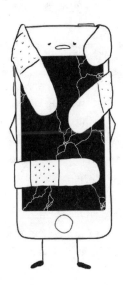

WHAT ARE SOME WARNING SIGNS THAT YOU OR SOMEONE YOU KNOW IS IN AN UNHEALTHY RELATIONSHIP?

There are a lot of different warning signs that someone might be in an unhealthy relationship. Signs could include their partner yelling or fighting with them a lot, looking through their private messages, demanding passwords, following them, hurting them, not letting them spend time with friends or family, or giving them no time apart. A really important sign that people don't always think about is that feeling a person gets in their stomach. You know, the one that says "something isn't right." Even if it seems like it's not a big deal, it's important to listen to that feeling. Both people should feel safe and comfortable in the relationship. If you or a friend are concerned about an unhealthy relationship, it's important to talk to a trusted adult.

IS TIME APART GOOD FOR A RELATIONSHIP?

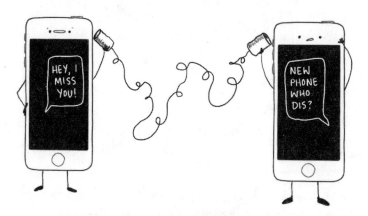

Just like spending time together in a relationship is important, so is having freedom and independence. Everyone deserves to have alone time, time with friends and family, and time to do their own thing—and so does their partner! It is common that both partners want to spend every possible moment together at the beginning of a relationship, and as people get more comfortable, they may start spending more time apart. That is normal and healthy. Some people need or want more time apart than others, and that is also normal and healthy. Talking about what feels right for each person helps everyone feel good in their relationship.

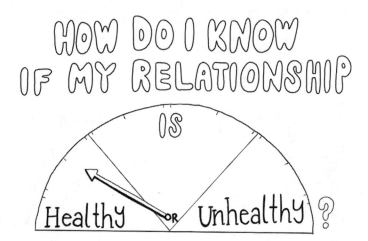

HOW DO I KNOW IF MY RELATIONSHIP IS Healthy OR Unhealthy?

A healthy relationship is not just rainbows and sunshine all the time. Every relationship looks different, but a healthy relationship should include trust, communication, and respect (and maybe some puppies). It's important that partners communicate honestly, share feelings (both good and bad), and respect each other's limits, boundaries, opinions, feelings, and privacy. Even in healthy relationships, there may be times when you argue, disagree, or just need some alone time. These things are also healthy as long as everyone feels respected! Everyone deserves to be in a relationship that makes them feel safe and happy (even on those rainy days).

WHAT IF THE GIRL IS THE ABUSIVE ONE?

Anyone can be abusive, regardless of their **gender**. No matter who is doing the abusing, it is never okay, and it's important to get support and help if you feel you're being abused. Abuse can be physical, mental, emotional, and sexual. No one deserves to be in an abusive relationship.

HOW CAN I ASK FOR HELP IN A SITUATION WHERE A PERSON MAKES ME FEEL UNSAFE?

If you are feeling unsafe or threatened in the moment, first try to see if there is support near you. If there are other people around, go directly to them and ask for help. If there is no one around, try to calmly leave the situation or call the police. Something doesn't have to physically happen to you to make a situation bad/uncomfortable/unsafe. Whenever you feel unsafe or scared (even if something just feels off or doesn't feel right), it's important to reach out for support and tell an adult you trust. Remember that feeling in your

stomach that says "this isn't right"? Again, it is okay to listen to that feeling, even if what's happening doesn't seem like a "big deal." No matter what happens, you are not at fault—only the person who is being threatening is at fault.

There are different reasons *why* someone might abuse someone else, including a desire to have power, a desire to control their partner, or their own insecurity. People who abuse might try to make the person they are hurting feel like it's their own fault; they might do this by blaming the person for making them angry, or they might say they are hurting the person because they **love** them. Remember, abuse is *never okay* in any situation, and if you're being abused, know that it is not your fault.

WHY DON'T PEOPLE JUST LEAVE ABUSIVE RELATIONSHIPS?

This isn't easy to answer. People stay in relationships for many different reasons. Leaving a relationship isn't always simple. Abusive relationships often follow the same patterns, with moments of deep **love** and connection (honeymoon), followed by tension building and an abusive explosion. This cycle often repeats itself again and again. People might stay in abusive and unhealthy relationships because of fear, lack of outside support, lack of money, emotional trauma, and so many other reasons. We should never judge a person in this type of relationship. What people in abusive relationships need more than anything is support from friends and family. If you notice a friend in a relationship that isn't safe, or if a friend tells you they are being abused, talking to a trusted adult is important. Even if a friend asks you not to tell, it is important to get support both for yourself and for your friend. Support can look like talking to a trusted adult, calling a hotline, or talking to the police.

Cycle of Abuse

Honeymoon

THE CYCLE OF VIOLENCE

EXPLOSION

TENSION BUILDING

MY GIRLFRIEND DOESN'T WANT ME TO HANG OUT WITH OTHER GIRLS, EVEN FRIENDS. IS THAT OK?

You have a right to have other friends, no matter their **gender**, and to have those relationships respected. Trying to control who a partner hangs out with could be a sign of **jealousy**.

Jealousy is a human emotion that almost everyone will feel in their lives. (Like when you see your two best friends are hanging out without you!) We can't always control how we feel, but we can control what we do about those feelings. Spending time with and having other friends is not only healthy for you, but it is also a sign of trust and respect in a relationship. If you feel uncomfortable, or don't like that your partner has made this request, it's important to talk to them about it.

SHOULD I GIVE MY PARTNER MY PASSWORDS?

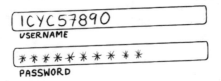

Depends. If your password is SlipperyBaNaNa2032, maybe don't share it because it's embarrassing. But really, we all use passwords to protect our privacy and personal information. Whether you decide to share your passwords with a partner is your choice. In some relationships partners share passwords, and in others they don't. It's never okay for someone to demand your passwords if you aren't comfortable giving them out. You have the right to keep your password private if you wish. If you are deciding whether you want to share your passwords, it's important to think about why your partner is asking. If they are asking because they don't trust that you're doing what you say, then it may be helpful to have a deeper conversation about what trust means to each of you. If they are asking because the random choice of SlipperyBaNaNa2032 as a password is a deal breaker, then that's different. Either way, you get to decide what is comfortable to you.

CAN I GET IN TROUBLE FOR PRESSURING SOMEONE?

Yes. If someone pressures another person to do something sexual, then they can get in big trouble with the law, with school, and/or at home. It is never okay to pressure someone—that's wrong. When someone gives consent (says "yes" to sexual activities including touching and kissing), it has to be freely given. If it's not freely given, then it's not consent. Having conversations about what you want, what you don't want, and each person's boundaries is necessary in healthy relationships. But once someone sets their boundaries, it is important to respect them. If their boundaries don't match what you are looking for in a relationship, then you can decide if that is the right relationship for you. If it is not the right relationship for you, then that is okay! If it is the right relationship for you, then you are accepting the boundaries your partner is setting.

Check out the consent chapter to learn more!

Someone asked me out and I don't want to say YES but I don't want to hurt their feelings. What do I do?

That's never fun. Only you know what is right for you in terms of who you date, and it's always okay to say no. It's possible that saying no may hurt their feelings, but that isn't enough of a reason to do something that doesn't feel right for you. No one wants to go out with someone who only said yes because they felt bad. Eventually you would have to be honest about your feelings, and it is much kinder to do it right away. Your feelings matter too. Some examples of how to turn down a date are, "I'm sorry, but I'm not interested," "No thank you," and "I like hanging out with you as a friend—can we keep doing that instead?" Being upfront and assertive with your feelings doesn't mean that you are being unkind.

WHY **DO** BROKEN HEARTS HURT SO BADLY?

Broken hearts hurt because a person is dealing with the reality that things aren't how they want them to be. For example, maybe someone didn't like them back, they're dealing with a breakup, or they miss someone. Almost everyone will feel broken-hearted at some point in their lives. Some people describe feeling a physical pain in their chest, like their heart actually hurts. Many people have a range of emotions: sad, angry, disappointed, irritable, relieved, confused, and so many more. And these feelings may change day to day, or even hour to hour, and usually get a little easier with time. Sometimes people don't want to be broken up, which could be especially difficult, and sometimes they do, but they still care about the other person. These emotions can feel very intense, sometimes overwhelming. If it ever feels overwhelming, it can help to talk or write about your feelings. Even though breakups can be hard, it's important to respect each other's decisions.

Tips for handling a breakup:
- *Don't hold your feelings inside—find a trusted person to talk to*
- *Hang out with friends*
- *Ice cream*
- *Give yourself some space from the ex*
- *More ice cream (unless you're lactose intolerant and then . . . cookies?)*

WHEN DO I KNOW IF I SHOULD END IT OR STAY WITH MY BOYFRIEND?

Wouldn't it be nice if a relationship was like a video game where you can hit reset? But that's not how it works, and we can't just start all over. So when deciding if your relationship has about run out of lives, a good place to start is to think about if you're happy and if you're getting what you want from the partnership. It's okay to want to end the relationship even if you can't put your finger on why. Sometimes it can help to talk it out. This may mean talking with your partner, to find out how they're feeling about the relationship, or with your friends or family, to get their opinions. Relationships take a lot of work, and sometimes you have to decide if it's worth it to you to keep working through an issue. In some relationships it is very clear why things aren't working, and in some it's not. Romantic relatationships are relationships we get to choose to be in. In the end, whether you stay in the relationship is up to you.

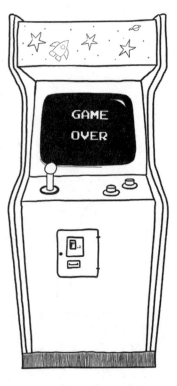

WHAT SHOULD YOU DO IF YOU LIKE A BOY AND YOUR FRIEND DOES TOO?

Yep, this can be difficult. You can't control who you're attracted to (and neither can your friend), but you can control what you do about it. When you have a crush, you can choose to keep it to yourself, share it with someone, or tell the person you have a crush on. When you and your friend have the same crush, it can make it much more complicated. It can help to talk to your friend about your feelings and what you want to do next, and listen to their reaction. Depending on what you decide, it is possible that it could change your relationship with your friend. No matter what you decide, it's important that you and your friend are respectful of each other.

WHAT IS LOVE?

Romantic **love** isn't easy to define. Most people would say it is a strong feeling of caring or desire for another person. Some signs that a person is in **love** include thinking about the person often, being attracted to them, and feeling excited to be around them (sometimes nervous, too). But, every single person can feel **love** and experience **love** in different ways! Talking to someone you trust, like a friend or family member, can help you sort out what you're feeling.

WILL SOMEONE EVER HAVE FEELINGS FOR ME?

Guess what—every person wonders this at some point in their life, and honestly, whether you know it or not, someone has probably had a crush on you (or will eventually). When that happens, you might like them, too, or you might not. Likewise, you might have a crush on someone, and they don't feel the same way about you. It can hurt when someone doesn't return our feelings, but we cannot make someone have feelings for us. Hang in there, you will find someone. Everyone deserves to be with someone who feels the same about them.

It can be really difficult to not feel supported in your relationship. However, you get to decide what's best for you and whether you stay in a relationship with your partner. Sometimes friends and family may see things in our relationship that we don't. Often the adults in our lives have more experience with relationships and can give us insight and advice. They may notice controlling behavior, **jealousy**, or other things that might be unhealthy. It can be helpful to talk to them about their concerns. This can also provide an opportunity for you to let them know how you feel about your partner, and how they can support you. Often these people just want what is best for you.

CHAPTER NINE

"HOW DO I TELL MY PARTNER NO?"

AND OTHER QUESTIONS ABOUT CONSENT

Trigger Warning

Talking about consent and **sexual abuse** can cause many emotions. This chapter covers topics about physical, emotional, and **sexual abuse**. Please take care of yourself when reading, and talk to a trusted adult if you need support. For resources, visit pages 263-264.

Simply put: consent is giving permission. In more detail, consent is saying "yes" to a sexual activity. It's important to get someone's consent without using **coercion** (force). An easy way to remember consent is to think about fries. Yeah, like what you eat! FRIES stands for:

F: Freely given (free from pressure, influence, or threat). Consent should always be freely given. If you feel pressured or feel like someone is forcing you or trying to convince you to do something you don't want to do, then you are not freely giving consent. You should be excited to do the activity, not reluctant!

R: Reversible (consent yesterday doesn't mean consent today, and people can change their mind whenever they want).

That's right, you can say "yes" to a certain sexual activity and then change your mind and never do that activity again, or you can decide to skip that activity and do something else instead. Guess what? You can even change your mind in the middle of a certain sexual activity and ask your partner to stop, and they need to listen to you.

I: Informed (people know what they are agreeing to with *all* the information they need before saying yes—this also means sober and awake). Yes, you read that right—sober. Sober means that everyone involved understands what is going to happen, can talk about what they want and don't want, and can inform the other person when they want to stop.

E: Enthusiastic (sexual consent should be given happily, where both people are into it and feel good about it). An enthusiastic yes is the best yes!

S: Specific (consent for each act, each time). Yep. Each and every time.[36]

Here are some ideas of ways to get consent:
▸ *Do you like it?*
▸ *How does this feel?*
▸ *I really want to _____, what do you think?*

F.R.I.E.S.

CAN SOMEONE CHANGE THEIR MIND EVEN AFTER THEY AGREED TO HAVE SEX?

Absolutely. **Sex** should only happen if both people want it to happen. A person has the right to change their mind at any time, including when they have already agreed to **sex** or when they have already started having **sex**. If a person says no, they must be respected, and all sexual contact should stop immediately.

WE HAVE SEX A LOT...
DO I REALLY HAVE TO ASK
FOR CONSENT
EVERY TIME?

Consent is how a person knows if their partner feels comfortable and is into, or engaged with, the sexual experience. Every relationship should include respect. So making sure that both partners want to have **sex**, *every time*, shows respect for each other. Getting and giving consent to **sex** can look different for different couples, so figuring out what works for you and your partner(s) is equally important. Keep in mind that just because a person said "yes" one time (or hundreds of times) doesn't mean they will say "yes" the next time. Sometimes people may feel tired, stressed, or just not that into it—and the only way to know for sure is to ask them!

For foxy ways to ask for consent, check out Page 241!

Rape is **sex** without consent. Any time a person forces another person to do anything sexual that they do not want to do, it is **sexual assault**, which can include **rape**. **Sexual assault** can happen to any **gender**, by any **gender**. It is never okay if anyone makes a person do something sexual that they do not want to do. Even if a person seems "turned on," that does not mean they want to have **sex**. An erect **penis** or a wet **vagina** doesn't mean a person wants to do the activity—this is just a natural bodily reaction, and reactions are not consent. All boundaries should be respected, every time.

HOW DO I TELL MY PARTNER NO?

It's important to say what you want and don't want when it comes to sexual activity. Some people find it empowering to say no, and other people may feel anxious about it or avoid it. Practicing how you say "no" in different scenarios can be really helpful. "Can you please stop," "I'm not comfortable with this," or, "No, that's not what I want right now," are all clear ways to let your partner know you want them to stop. Sometimes saying "no" means stopping what you're doing all together, deciding not to move forward, or taking a step back. If you want to say "no" but you need a little extra time to figure out how to say it, you can buy yourself some time by using a delay tactic. Excusing yourself to the bathroom or stepping out to make a phone call can put things on pause until you're ready to talk. Just remember, you deserve to have your boundaries respected and you have every right to say "no," even if it's to someone you care about. If someone violates your boundaries or you need some extra help, check out the Wrap Up section for some additional resources.

If someone says no to you, whatever activity is happening needs to stop immediately. It is not okay to continue, to try to get them to change their answer, or to threaten them. It is always important to respect your partner's boundaries.

WHAT WOULD YOU DO IF SOMEONE PRESSURED YOU TO HAVE SEX?

It is *never* okay for anyone to pressure a person to have **sex**. In fact, it's against the law. Everyone deserves to have a partner that respects their boundaries. If someone is trying to pressure you, you have the right to leave the situation. What they are doing is wrong, and you do not have to do anything you don't want to do. If someone is pressuring you or has not respected your boundaries, finding a trusted adult or counselor to talk with can be really helpful. A trusted adult can help you form a plan for what to do next. Some trusted adults may want to just talk about what happened, others may want to make a police report. Just remember, because forcing someone to have **sex** is illegal, a police report may need to be made (depending on what happened, the person's age, and the state laws). No matter what you choose, know that it is not your fault.

There are many people beyond police officers who can help you report abuse. Depending on the state you live in, some people's jobs may even require them to report any abuse of a person under 18.

WHY IS IT SO HARD TO STOP WHEN WE START MAKING OUT?

Making out can feel really good, and can be sexually arousing. Sometimes when something feels good, it's hard to stop. Think about when you're eating your favorite type of cookie—it can be really hard to stop eating them, right? Knowing and deciding what you are and aren't comfortable doing sexually before you start making out can help you know when to slow down. If you find yourself in a situation and you're feeling confused, you can always stop touching and kissing to think about what you want to do in that moment. Take a minute to think—you can even say you need to go to the bathroom to give yourself some time to figure out what you want to do. It can also be hard to tell someone "no" if you like them because you worry about hurting their feelings. But your feelings and boundaries are just as important as theirs; and no one should make you feel like your boundaries are not important.

Who hasn't had a moment where they think, "What am I do-ing? Why did I say 'yes' to this?" (Like that date where you went rock climbing but you're afraid of heights.) Having a crush can make us do some silly things and push us out of our comfort zone. When you want someone to like you, or you want to impress them, it can be hard to think clearly because of all the adrenaline and hormones flying around inside you, especially when those feelings are exciting and feel good. It might also be hard to say "no" if you don't want to make the other person upset, or if you're not sure what sexual activities you're comfortable with. So when you say "yes" to a sexual activity, you should make sure you know what you're getting in to. You should also know how to stay safe while taking new sexual risks. Wow, that's a lot to consider. Thinking about what you are or are not comfortable with before diving head first into a new relationship can be really helpful in being able to stick to your boundaries.

what if someone **gets MAD** AT YOU FOR saying NO?

Remember, it is always okay to say "no!" And when you say, "no," you deserve to be respected. Of course, when you say "no," your partner might get upset or frustrated. And that's okay too. But, if someone gets mad when you say "no" and makes you feel unsafe, leave the situation immediately if you can and consider calling someone for help. (If you feel like you are in real danger, don't hesitate to call 911.) If you are talking about a partner that just gets frustrated or annoyed when you say "no," remember that you deserve to always have your boundaries respected. If they care about your needs as much as they care about their own, your partner might get mad, but they will get over it and show you the respect you deserve. Stay true to you. If your partner does not get over feeling frustrated, and does not show you respect and kindness, you might want to consider whether this is the best relationship for you. Either way, don't change your mind because someone gets mad at you.

WHAT DO YOU DO IF YOU GET A NUDE?

Whoa, maybe you didn't expect to see *that*! Some people send nude pictures out of the blue, and some people might try and send them as a way of flirting. No matter what, if a person receives a nude and that person is under the age of 18, it is against the law. If the person in the picture is under 18, it is also against the law. And guess what, forwarding that picture (even to your best friend) is against the law. If you get a nude, your best bet is to talk with a trusted adult immediately to stay safe.

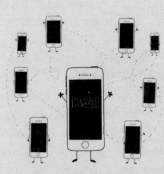

Sometimes it's called **sexting** when people send naked photos. But remember, you can't control what happens to those pictures after you push send. Any time you send something or post online, it's a good idea to think about who might see it, what's going on in the post, and whether there's anything in the post that could feel uncomfortable to you or someone else.

IF TWO PEOPLE ARE DRINKING, DOES THAT MEAN THEY CAN'T HAVE SEX?

Being sober ensures that people know what they are saying yes to and their judgment isn't clouded. Remember consent and FRIES (page 241)? To be able to enthusiastically consent to a sexual activity, people should be able to understand what they are saying "yes" to. This is not always possible when people are drunk or high. Not to mention, depending on the state you are in, it may be against the law! And remember, in every state, drinking alcohol or using recreational marijuana under the age of 21 is also against the law.

DO MEN TAKE ADVANTAGE OF WOMEN BECAUSE THEY WANT IT OR THEY'RE DRUNK?

Power, control, and insecurity are some of the reasons why people, not just men, might take advantage of another person, or cross another person's boundaries (more examples of how people abuse power and control are on the wheel below). Some people say that being drunk makes them do things they wouldn't do normally. Whatever the reason, it's no excuse. It's never okay to cross someone's sexual boundaries.

HOW CAN I ASK FOR CONSENT SO THAT IT IS NOT AWKWARD?

Asking for consent can be comfortable (and even sexy!). Knowing that you and your partner are both okay with what's going on can help you feel more relaxed and confident so that you both enjoy it more. Consent is as easy as asking someone if they want to do something, or if they're good with what is happening. It does not have to be a long conversation, but it does have to happen.

Sexy Suggestions:

▶ Do you want to go do _____?

▶ How would you feel if I did _____ to you?

▶ Does that feel good?

▶ Do you like that?

▶ Are you okay?

IF I SEE SOMETHING THAT IS NOT CONSENSUAL, HOW DO I HELP?

It can be difficult to tell from far away if someone is giving another person consent or not. A person refusing consent could look like a person pulling away and looking uncomfortable, a person being unconscious or drunk, or a person verbally telling someone "no" and/or even pushing them away. Sometimes it might feel awkward to step in, but if what is happening is making you uncomfortable, or if you know it's wrong, it's important to check in with the person and make sure they are okay. If the situation isn't safe, go get help. This is called bystander intervention.

Tips for intervening as a bystander:[37]

▶ *Be direct. Ask someone who looks like they may need help if they're okay or if they need any help.*

▶ *Get someone to help you if you see something.*

▶ *Get in the way by creating a distraction, drawing attention to the situation, or separating them.*

WHAT DOES THE LAW SAY ABOUT CONSENT?

Every state has a different law about consent. If you want to know your state's law, you can find it here: https://apps.rainn.org/policy/. Some states have laws about how old a person has to be to give consent, how old their partner has to be, and/or the relationship between partners. It is important that before a person starts a sexual relationship they know the laws and how those laws can affect their decisions.

No, really, the laws are really different for each state. For example, all states have an **age of consent**, but some states also have rules about how big a gap there can be between partners' ages when they are underage. Whereas other states have rules saying people under a certain age can't consent to any sexual activity no matter how old their partner is.

WRAP UP

You did it! You got through all the questions in this book! Or you just flipped to the back and started reading—either way, we are thrilled. Answering questions is the best part of our jobs at ICYC. ICYC makes sure that the information people actually want gets to them when they need it. While the questions we put in this book cover a lot of information, we know we couldn't answer everything. So below you will find a few extras to help connect you even further to answers and support.

First, you will find some conversation starters. It's likely you noticed that we kept telling you to go talk with people—trusted adults, friends, and partners. You might be thinking, "How do I do that? What would I say?" Those are great questions to be asking yourself, and this next section is for you. If you're still feeling like you need more support, you can always text "ICYC?" to 57890 or visit our Instagram page @incaseyourecurious.

After the conversation starters, you will see links for resources that relate to all of the chapters of the book. These links can help continue the learning started here. Finally, the book ends with a glossary, so if there were any words you didn't know in the book, or if you just want to explore terms related to sexual health, go and take a look.

So now you're finishing up your *ICYC* book experience. What's the big takeaway? *ICYC* wants you to remember, even if it's the only thing you remember, **you deserve to have your questions answered, and we are here for you.** Thanks for reading, and text us any time.

CONVERSATION STARTERS:

How do I talk to my parent or guardian?

▶ "So I was wondering if we could talk and I could ask you about my relationship."

▶ "Hey, Dad, I have a question about my period and I don't feel comfortable talking to anyone but you."

▶ "Well, this is uncomfortable but I want your opinion, how do I know when I'm ready to have sex?"

How do I talk to my partner?

▶ "It's really important for me to feel like my partner cares about me, so I like to talk on the phone together once a day. Does that work for you?"

▶ "I know we've been hanging out a lot. I really like you and wanted to know if we could start being exclusive?"

▶ "I really care about our relationship, and I need you to know that I don't like it when you assume every time we see each other that we are going to have sex."

While texting may be your favorite way to check in with someone, it's best to have the big conversations face-to-face. No one likes to get the "We should talk" text.

How do I talk to a doctor?

▸ "I know you do this for a living, but it's hard for me to talk about my body. Can I ask you about how to do a breast exam?"

▸ "I want to make sure I understand correctly, can you tell me how this medicine works again?"

▸ "I'm pretty nervous about this exam. Can you talk me through everything you're going to do?"

Talking about pregnancy:

▸ "Hey, so I wanted to ask you how you would feel if we were to get pregnant?"

▸ "Do you feel like you're ready to be a parent?"

▸ "I am ready to have sex but I don't want to have a kid, what would we do if we got pregnant?"

Conversations about pregnancy, pregnancy prevention, and STI prevention are best had before people have sex.

Talking about LGBTQ+/ Identity:

- "I actually use they/them pronouns."

- "I'm so glad you felt comfortable telling me that, I want you to know I support you and respect your privacy."

- "I understand that you're curious, but I don't feel like explaining my identity right now."

Remember that an important part of health care is finding a doctor who respects and understands your needs. Check out this link for steps to finding an LGBTQ+ supportive health care provider: http://www.thecentersd.org/pdf/health-advocacy/how-to-find-and-lgbt-friendly.pdf.

Talking about testing:

- "Before we have sex, I wanted to know if you have any sexually transmitted infections?"

- "When was the last time you got tested?"

- "I was thinking we could go get tested together, what do you think?"

Talking about birth control:

- "I know I'm not ready for a child, so how are we going to protect ourselves from pregnancy when we have sex?"

- "Since we both don't want an unexpected pregnancy, I think we should share the cost of birth control."

- "I think we should use a condom even though I'm on the pill because it protects against STIs."

Talking about sex:

- ▸ "I'm not ready to have sex yet. How can I show you that I care in another way?"
- ▸ "What are you comfortable with doing right now?"
- ▸ "Before we have sex, I want to be clear that you're not my only partner."

ANATOMY LINKS:

https://kidshealth.org/en/teens/female-repro.html
> Teen-friendly site that explains anatomy for a person with a vagina. Includes slide show with drawings and labels. Available in English and Spanish.

https://kidshealth.org/en/teens/male-repro.html
> Teen friendly site that explains anatomy for a person with a penis. Includes slide show with drawings and labels. Available in English and Spanish.

https://www.youtube.com/watch?v=1xPZqe_0Z5Y
> "Different is Normal" video created by Planned Parenthood. Your body is confusing, especially during puberty. You don't need to worry about whether your breasts, penis, vagina, or any other parts of your body are normal. Each person's body is different—and different is normal.

http://teentalksa.org/sex/anatomy/
> In order to understand anything about sex, it is important that you are familiar with human anatomy. More

specifically, the male and female reproductive system. By understanding your body, you are more in control of what happens to it.

STI LINKS:

https://www.plannedparenthood.org/learn/stds-hiv-safer-sex

Youth-friendly site with general information about STIs, with ability to click to get further information about specific STIs. Includes a short video. Available in English and Spanish.

http://teenhealthsource.com/stisetc/7053/

Teen-centered site that offeres general information about STIs. This site also offers the ability to connect and talk to a trained teen volunteer.

https://beforeplay.org/stds/

Sex-positive site that normalizes sexual health and open, honest conversations with your partner(s). Although conversations about birth control, STIs, and pregnancy aren't really at the top of every young person's list to talk about, beforeplay.org believes they should be. Available in English and Spanish.

RELATIONSHIPS LINKS:

https://www.loveisrespect.org/healthy-relationships/

> Loveisrespect.org is geared to teens. The site is an ultimate resource to empower youth to prevent and end dating abuse. Wondering if you are in a healthy relationship? Take their quiz. Available in English and Spanish.

http://www.athinline.org/

> MTV's A Thin Line campaign was developed to empower youth to identify, respond to, and stop the spread of digital abuse in their lives and among their peers. The campaign is built on the understanding that there's a "thin line" between what may begin as a harmless joke and something that could end up having a serious impact on an individual. Available in English and Spanish.

https://www.plannedparenthood.org/teens/relationships/relationships-101

> How do I know if a crush likes me back? How do I ask someone out? This site asks these questions and helps you get answers! Available in English and Spanish.

www.thehotline.org

> Operating around the clock, seven days a week, confidential and free of cost, the National Domestic Violence Hotline provides lifesaving tools and immediate support to enable victims to find safety and live lives free of abuse. Available in English and Spanish.

PUBERTY LINKS:

http://kidshealth.org/en/teens/puberty.html

>Youth-friendly site that discusses puberty and all the changes that happen. Includes additional questions youth might have about puberty. Available in English and Spanish.

https://www.plannedparenthood.org/teens/my-body/puberty

>Defines puberty, and discusses changes that happen, emotional experiences, and healthy ways to handle it all. Includes videos, a glossary of terms, and additional questions youth might have. Available in English and Spanish.

https://www.medicinenet.com/puberty/article.htm#puberty_facts

>Information for adults to support their youth as they transition through puberty; includes terms and puberty facts.

CONSENT LINKS:

https://www.youtube.com/watch?v=fGoWLWS4-kU&feature=youtu.be

>"Consent is as simple as tea." A cartoon video that describes how understanding consent is as easy as understanding if a person wants tea or not.

https://www.youtube.com/watch?v=qNN3nAevQKY&feature=youtu.be

>Video discussing the importance of consent. The only

way to know if someone wants to have sex with you is to ask. Consent is about asking, and listening to the answer.

https://amaze.org/?topic=healthy-relationships

Youth-friendly videos about healthy relationships, puberty, pregnancy, STIs, and so much more. Digital media to provide children, adolescents, parents, and educators with medically accurate, affirming, and honest sexual health information along with free, engaging resources that can be accessed anytime, anywhere—regardless of where they live or what school they attend. Currently available in five languages, with more to come.

PREGNANCY LINKS:

https://www.plannedparenthood.org/learn/teens/preventing-pregnancy-stds/i-think-im-pregnant-now-what

How do I know if I'm pregnant? What do I do now? Answers to these questions and more. Offers the ability to talk directly to someone at Planned Parenthood and make an appointment from the website.

http://www.cyh.com/HealthTopics/HealthTopicDetailsKids.aspx?id=1613&np=289&p=335

Website for kids, with a section for pre-teens. Information about all health topics, including sexual reproduction. Includes drawings to help with understanding.

https://www.livescience.com/44899-stages-of-pregnancy.html

> Geared for upper teens to adults. Extensive description of conception, development, and birth.

SEXUAL IDENTITY/GENDER IDENTITY/ SEXUAL ORIENTATION LINKS:

www.glsen.org

> Mission is to create safe and affirming schools for all, regardless of sexual orientation, gender identity, or gender expression.

www.hrc.org

> Human Rights Campaign is the largest national lesbian, gay, bisexual, transgender, and queer civil rights organization. HRC envisions a world where LGBTQ+ people are ensured of their basic equal rights, and can be open, honest, and safe at home, at work, and in the community.

https://www.plannedparenthood.org/teens/lgbtq

> Definitions, questions, and answers for teens about LGBTQ+ topics. Available in English and Spanish.

BIRTH CONTROL LINKS:

https://www.plannedparenthood.org/learn/birth-control

> Birth control is how you prevent pregnancy. There are lots of different birth control options out there. This site helps a person figure it all out by helping

them decide what's important in their birth control choice. Available in English and Spanish.

https://www.bedsider.org/methods
Pictures of all available birth control methods that can be catorgized by most effective, hormone free, STI prevention, etc. Hover over the picture of the method to learn more.

https://fc2femalecondom.com/
Learn about the female condom, how to use it, where to get it, and order it online. Available in the United States and globally.

http://stayteen.org/sex-ed/birth-control-explorer
Site is geared specifically for teens and sorts birth control methods by what is most effective or non-hormonal, and whether you need a doctor's appointment.

GENERAL INFO LINKS:

https://responsiblesexedinstitute.org/
You like this book, you will like this site. It is about us, the Planned Parenthood of the Rocky Mountains educators. Information for parents, teens, and educators. Come have a look and see how we can support you.

https://texticyc.com/
Want to learn more about ICYC, where we are located, and how to contact us? Look no further—this is the place.

https://www.instagram.com/incaseyourecurious/?hl=en

Are you a little bit curious about the other questions teens ask that didn't make it into the book? Take a look at our Instagram page. You can even comment and get a response to any question posted.

https://plannedparenthood.org/

Wonder what Planned Parenthood does? Learn about our health services, education, advocacy, and so much more. Visit our website to learn more or to make an appointment. Available in English and Spanish.

http://pprm.org

Information about the incredible Planned Parenthood of the Rocky Mountains. Learn about us and make an appointment.

GLOSSARY

(Glossary created by Planned Parenthood Federation of America 9.28.18)

A:

Abortion: Ending a **pregnancy**.

Abortion pill: Describes the process of **medication abortion**, which includes the use of two medications, mifepristone and misoprostol, to safely end a **pregnancy**.

Abstinence: Not having **sex** with anyone.

Ace: Short for asexual, meaning the **sexual orientation**, or spectrum of identities, associated with experiencing no sexual attraction towards anyone.

Acquaintance rape: **Sexual assault** by someone the victim knows.

Adolescence: The **period** of physical and emotional change between the beginning of **puberty** and early adulthood.

Age of consent: The age at which state law considers a person old enough to decide to have **sex** with someone.

Agender: Not identifying with any **gender**.

AIDS (acquired immune deficiency syndrome): The most advanced stage of **HIV**.

Ally: Someone who's on the same side as you. Often used to describe someone who takes a stand against oppression or discrimination who is not a member of the oppressed group — for example, a white person who speaks out against racism or a **straight** person who speaks out against **homophobia**.

Anal sex: **Sex** in which the **penis** or a **sex** toy goes in the anus.

Androgynous: Appearing to have both, neither, or in between traditionally male and female physical characteristics.

Antibiotics: Medicines that are used to cure infections caused by bacteria.

Asymptomatic: Having no signs or symptoms. Many **STIs** are asymptomatic in their early stages.

B:

Backup birth control: Any **birth control** method—like **condoms** or **withdrawal**—that's used while waiting for hormonal **birth control** methods to become effective (or to become effective again after a mistake or problem). Some people also refer to **emergency contraception** as backup **birth control**.

Bacterial vaginosis (bv): Inflammation of the **vulva/vagina** (vaginitis) caused by a change in the balance of **vaginal** bacteria. It's not an **STI**. Things like douching or having **sex** with a new partner can lead to BV.

Barrier methods of birth control: **Birth control** that blocks **sperm** from passing through the **cervix** (the barrier between the **vagina** and **uterus**). These include the **condom**, female **condom**, diaphragm, cervical cap, spermicide, and sponge.

Bigender: Having two **genders**. Identifying as both a man and a woman, for example.

Birth canal: The passage from the **uterus** through the **cervix** and **vagina** through which a baby is born.

Birth control: Something that prevents **pregnancy**.

Bisexual: Being sexually attracted to both men and women. Sometimes used to describe people who are sexually attracted to people of all **genders**, including **non-binary genders**.

Bladder: The organ that collects and stores urine (pee). The bladder is emptied through the **urethra**.

Blue balls: Slang for an uncomfortable—but not danger-ous—feeling in the **penis/testicles** that may occur when you don't ejaculate after being very turned on.

Body image: Attitudes and feelings that a person has about their body and appearance.

Boner: Slang for an erect (hard) **penis**.

Breastfeeding: Feeding a baby with human milk from the breast. Can also be used as a **birth control** method for the first 6 months after birth, if done correctly.

Breasts: The two glands on the chest. Considered **sex** or-gans because they're often sexually sensitive and may in-spire sexual desire. Like mammary glands in other mam-mals, they produce milk during and after **pregnancy**.

C:

C-section: Giving birth when a doctor surgically removes the baby from the **uterus**. Short for caesarian section.

Casual sex: **Sex** between people who aren't in a relationship with each other.

Celibacy: Not having **sex**.

Censorship: When something is forbidden because it's thought to be offensive or dangerous.

Cervical mucus: The secretion that comes from the divider between the **uterus** and **vagina**. The amount of cervical mucus and what it looks like changes throughout the **men-strual cycle**, especially around the time of **ovulation**. It can naturally help **sperm** move, or help stop **sperm** from moving if you're using hormonal **birth control**.

Cervix: The narrow, lower part of the **uterus**, with a small opening connecting the **uterus** to the **vagina**.

Chest binding: Wrapping breast tissue in order to flatten it and create a more **masculine**-appearing chest.

Child pornography: Images of children designed to be sexually arousing. Making, distributing, and consuming **child pornography** are serious crimes.

Chlamydia: A very common **STI** that's caused by a bacteria and can be cured with **antibiotics**. If left untreated, **chlamydia** can cause **infertility** and arthritis.

Circumcision: A surgical procedure to remove the foreskin of the **penis** or part of the **clitoris**.

Cis man: Short for **cisgender** man. A man who identifies as the **gender** he was assigned at birth—in this case, male. A man who isn't **transgender**.

Cis woman: Short for **cisgender** woman. A woman who identifies as the **gender** she was assigned at birth—in this case, female. A woman who isn't **transgender**.

Cisgender: Those who identify as the **gender** they were assigned at birth. For example, a baby born with a **vulva** is categorized a girl. If she also identifies as a girl or woman throughout her life, she's considered **cisgender**. In other words, **cisgender** describes someone who is not **transgender**.

Climax: An **orgasm** or to have an **orgasm**.

Clinician: A qualified health care professional, such as a doctor, nurse, **nurse practitioner**, or physician assistant. Also called "**health care provider**."

Clit: Short for clitoris.

Clitoral hood: A small flap of skin formed by the inner **labia** that covers and protects the **clitoris**.

Clitoris: **Sex** organ whose only known purpose is sexual pleasure. The **clitoris** swells with blood during sexual **excitement**. The outer part of the **clitoris** is located at the top/front of the **vulva**, right next to the **urethra** (hole you pee out of). The inner part of the **clitoris**, which is much larger, includes a **shaft** and two crura (roots or legs) of tissue that extend up to five inches into the body on both sides of the **vagina** to attach to the pubic bone.

Closet: "Being in the **closet**," or "being closeted," means not sharing or not being able to share your **LGBTQ+** identity with yourself or others.

Coercion: Forcing someone to do something they don't want to do, often with threats or emotional manipulation.

Combination pill: A **birth control pill** that contains two **hormones**: **estrogen** and progestin.

Combined hormone contraceptives: **Birth control** methods—**the pill**, the patch, the ring—that contain two **hormones**: **estrogen** and progestin.

Combined oral contraceptives: **Birth control pills** that contain two **hormones**: **estrogen** and progestin.

Coming out: The process of accepting and being open about one's identity, such as being **lesbian**, **gay**, **bisexual**, **transgender**, **queer**, or **questioning**. Short for "**coming out** of the **closet**."

Conception: The beginning of **pregnancy**. The moment when the **pre-embryo** attaches to the lining of the **uterus** and **pregnancy** begins.

Condom: Thin, stretchy pouch worn on the **penis** during **sex**. Mostly made from latex or plastics (like polyurethane and polyisoprene). Sometimes made from lambskin. **Condoms** are an **over-the-counter** barrier method of **birth control** that also provide protection from **STIs**, with one exception—lambskin **condoms** don't protect against **STIs**.

Contraception/contraceptive: Any behavior, device, medication, or procedure used to prevent **pregnancy**. Also known as **birth control**.

Contraction: The on-again, off-again tightening of the **uterus** during childbirth, which causes intense cramping.

Cowper's glands: Produce pre-ejaculate (AKA **precum**), a clear fluid that prepares the **urethra** for **ejaculation**. Pre-ejaculate also reduces friction in the **urethra**, making it easier for **semen** to pass through.

Cum: Slang for "ejaculate," the **sperm**-containing fluid that comes out of the **penis** usually during an **orgasm**. Also another way of saying "to have an **orgasm**."

Cybersex: Sexual encounters that take place online, using video cams, e-mail, or instant messaging.

Cyberstalking: To track and follow someone's online presence and communications in a threatening way.

D:

Date rape: Forced sexual contact from someone the victim knows or is dating. Also sometimes called "**acquaintance rape**."

Dental dam: A thin, square piece of latex that helps prevent the spread of **STIs** when placed over the **vulva** or anus during **oral sex**.

Depo-provera: The brand name of the **birth control** shot. The shot is a **hormone** that's injected into the butt or arm every three months to prevent **pregnancy**.

Desire phase: The first stage of the sexual response cycle.

Domestic partnership: A committed, long-term relationship of two unmarried people who live together.

Double standard: Unequal expectations, moral standards, or rules that allow one group to have more privileges than another group within a society. A sexual double standard, for example, usually places more restrictions on women than on men.

Douche: A spray of water, medication, or cleanser, which goes into the **vagina**.

Drag: Exaggerated cross-dressing for entertainment.

E:

Ectopic pregnancy: A life-threatening **pregnancy** that develops outside the **uterus**, often in a **fallopian tube**.

Egg: The **reproductive cell** stored in the **ovaries** and released during **ovulation**. **Pregnancy** happens when **sperm** enters an **egg**, grows into a ball of cells, and **implants** into the **uterus**.

Ejaculation: The moment when **semen** spurts out of the opening of the **urethra** in the **glans** of the **penis**.

Embryo: The organism that develops from a **pre-embryo** during the second month of **pregnancy**. This stage of the **pregnancy** lasts about five weeks. **Embryos** then develop into **fetuses**.

Emergency contraception: A safe and effective way to prevent **pregnancy** after unprotected **sex**. **Emergency contraception pills** made from **hormones** and copper **IUDs** are the two methods of **emergency contraception**.

Endometriosis: A condition in which endometrial tissue (the tissue that lines the **uterus**) grows outside the **uterus**, causing pain, especially before and during menstruation.

Epididymis: The tube that leads from the **testes** to the **vas deferens**. **Sperm** are stored in the **epididymis** before **ejaculation**. It's tightly coiled on top of and behind the **testes**.

Epidural: An injection of painkillers used during childbirth.

Erectile tissue: Spongy tissue in the **penis/clitoris** that stiffens when filled with blood.

Erection: A "hard" **penis**—when it becomes full of blood and stiffens. See "vasocongestion."

Erotic: Sexually arousing.

Estrogen: A **hormone** made in the **ovaries**, and in much smaller amounts in the adrenal glands at the top of your kidneys, and sometimes even in fat tissue. **Estrogen** plays a part in **puberty**, the **menstrual cycle**, and **pregnancy**. Many people take extra **estrogen** after **menopause** or as part of **transgender** care.

Excitement: The body's physical response to desire and to stimulation. The second stage of the sexual response cycle.

External sex and reproductive organs: The **sex** organs and structures that you can see. These include the **vulva**, **penis**, and **scrotum**.

F:

Fallopian tube: One of two narrow tubes that carry an **egg** from the **ovary** to the **uterus** during **ovulation**.

Family planning: Making plans and taking actions, like using **birth control**, to have the number of children you want, when you want them.

Female condom: A polyurethane pouch that goes inside the **vagina** or anus for **pregnancy** and/or **STI** prevention. **Female condoms** are sometimes called internal **condoms** or referred to by their brand name, FC2 **Female Condom**®.

Feminine: Characteristics and ways of appearing and behaving that a culture associates with being a girl or a woman.

Feminism: The belief that people of all **genders** should have equitable economic, political, sexual, and social rights.

Femme: An identity associated with a **gender** presentation that is considered "**feminine**."

Fertility: The ability to have children or cause a **pregnancy**.

Fertility cycle: Another way of saying the **menstrual cycle**. The monthly pattern of **ovulation**, the shedding of the lining of the **uterus** (menstruation), and the body's preparation for another **ovulation**.

Fertility rate: The number of live births per 1,000 women of reproductive age (15–44).

Fertilization: The joining of an **egg** and **sperm**.

Fetus: Develops from the **embryo** at 10 weeks of **pregnancy** and receives nourishment through the **placenta**.

First trimester: The first three months of **pregnancy**.

Foreplay: Kissing, rubbing, stroking, and/or touching that leads to **sex**. **Foreplay** can prolong and/or increase sexual **excitement** and pleasure.

Foreskin: A tube of skin that covers and protects the **glans** (head) of the **penis**, and rolls back when the **penis** becomes erect. A circumcised **penis** has had the foreskin removed.

G:

G-spot (Gräfenburg spot): An area inside the **vagina** that's highly sensitive to touch, along the upper wall of the **vagina**. Stimulation of the **G spot** can lead to intense **sexual arousal** and **orgasm** for some people.

Gay: When someone is only attracted to people of the same **gender**.

Gender: A social and legal status of male or female. A set of expectations from society about behaviors and characteristics. Each culture has standards about the way that people should behave based on whether they're male or female.

Gender affirming surgery: Surgery on **sex** organs or **secondary sex characteristics** to match one's **gender identity**.

Gender assignment: The medical and legal description of one's **sex**, determined at birth.

Gender binary: The idea that there are only two categories of **gender** (male and female) that are mutually exclusive and different from each other.

Gender fluidity: The flexibility of **gender** expressions and identities that may change over time or even from day to day. A **gender fluid** person may feel male on some days, female on others, both male and female, or neither. A **gender fluid** person might also identify as **genderqueer**.

Gender identity: An individual's inner feelings and outer expressions of their **gender**.

Gender nonconforming or non-binary: When a person's **gender** expression doesn't fit inside traditional male or female categories (sometimes called the **gender binary**). These labels can include someone who identifies as both male and female, neither male nor female, or some other **gender** altogether. It's not the same as being **transgender** and should only be used if someone self-identifies as **gender nonconforming or non-binary**.

Gender norms: Social standards on appropriate **feminine** and **masculine** behavior.

Gender roles: Social standards on appropriate **feminine** and **masculine** behavior.

Gender stereotype: Exaggerated expectations of the way boys/men or girls/women should behave.

Genderqueer: A term for people who don't identify as a man or a woman or whose identity lies outside the traditional **gender binary** of male and female. Some people use **genderqueer, gender nonconforming**, and **non-binary** interchangeably, but others don't. **Genderqueer** has a political history, so many use the term to identify their **gender** as non-normative in some way. For example, someone could identify as both **cisgender** female and **genderqueer**.

Genes: Microscopic chains in your cells that carry information about you that's unique to you, but includes pieces from your biological family—everything from eye color, to height, to body type, to personality.

Genital herpes: A common **STI** in the area of the anus, **cervix**, **penis**, **vagina**, or **vulva**. Very often there are no symptoms, while the most common symptom is a cluster of blistery sores. Since it's a virus, there is no cure, but there is treatment available.

Genital warts: Soft, flesh-colored growths on or near the **penis**/**vulva**, caused by some types of **HPV (human papilloma virus)**. They are usually painless, but may itch.

Genitals: External **sex** and **reproductive organs**, like the the **vulva**, **penis**, and **scrotum**.

Glans: The soft, highly sensitive tip of the **clitoris** or **penis**. Also called the "head" of the **penis**.

Gonorrhea: A bacterial **STI** that's easy to treat, but if left untreated can lead to **infertility**, arthritis, and heart problems. Often has no symptoms.

Gynecologist: A doctor who specializes in health care for the **vulva**, **vagina**, **uterus**, **ovaries**, and **breasts**.

H:

Health care provider: A licensed doctor, nurse, **nurse practitioner**, nurse-midwife, or physician assistant.

Health insurance: A plan or program that helps pay for the medical expenses of their members, like medicine, doctor visits, and surgery.

Heavy petting: Touching a partner's **genitals** in a sexual way.

Hepatitis b virus (HBV): A viral infection that can be sexually transmitted. It can lead to dangerous liver problems in some people.

Herpes: A common **STI** caused by two different but similar viruses: **herpes** simplex virus type 1 (HSV-1) and **herpes** simplex virus type 2 (HSV-2). Both kinds can make blistery sores show up on and around the **genitals** or mouth.

Heteronormativity: The cultural assumption that everyone is **straight** (**heterosexual**) until they tell you otherwise.

Heterosexism: The belief that **heterosexuality** is better than other **sexual orientations**.

Heterosexual: Being attracted to people of the other **gender**.

High-risk pregnancy: A **pregnancy** that is more likely to have complications for the pregnant person or their **fetus**.

HIV (human immunodeficiency virus): A chronic virus that breaks down the **immune system**. Can lead to **AIDS** if not treated.

Homophobia: Fear or hatred of people who are **gay**, **lesbian**, or **bisexual**.

Homosexual: Being attracted to people of the same **gender**.

Hormonal contraceptives: **Birth control** methods that use **hormones** to prevent **pregnancy**. These include the **implant**, the hormonal **IUD**, **the pill**, the patch, the ring, and the shot.

Hormones: Chemicals that cause changes in our bodies and brains. They naturally exist and can also be made in a lab.

Horny: Slang for wanting to have **sex** or for being sexually aroused.

HPV (human papilloma virus): The most common **STI**. Some types of **HPV** may cause **genital warts**. Others may cause cancer of the anus, **cervix**, **penis**, throat, or **vulva**. Most of the time **HPV** is harmless and goes away on its own.

Hymen: A thin, fleshy piece of tissue that stretches across part of the opening to the **vagina**.

Hysterectomy: Surgery to remove the **uterus**.

I:

Immune system: The body's natural protection against infection and disease.

Implant: A small rod, about the size of a matchstick, that prevents **pregnancy** for up to four years. A doctor or nurse inserts the **implant** under the skin of the upper arm. It releases the **hormone** progestin to prevent **pregnancy**.

Implantation: When a **pre-embryo** attaches to the lining of the **uterus**. This is when **pregnancy** begins. Usually starts about six days after **fertilization** (when **egg** and **sperm** meet) and takes three to four days to complete.

In vitro fertilization (IVF): Any method of assisted reproduction in which **fertilization** takes place outside the body (usually in a lab) in an effort to get someone pregnant.

In-clinic abortion: A procedure done in a health center, doctor's office, or hospital that ends a **pregnancy**.

Infatuation: Intense, usually short-lived, emotional or sexual attraction to another person.

Infertility: The inability to become pregnant or to cause a **pregnancy**.

Insemination: Putting **sperm** into the **vagina**, **cervix**, **uterus**, or **fallopian tubes** to cause a **pregnancy**.

Intact penis: A **penis** with a foreskin, also called uncircumcised.

Intercourse: Sexual activity in which the **penis** goes into the **vagina** (**vaginal intercourse**) or the anus (anal **intercourse**).

Internal sex and reproductive organs: The organs inside the body that are responsible for reproduction. **Internal reproductive organs** that respond to sexual stimulation (like the **vagina**) are also called **sex** organs.

Internalized homophobia: Fear of being **homosexual** or negative feelings towards oneself for being **homosexual**.

Intersex: A general term used for a variety of conditions in which a person is born with a reproductive or sexual anatomy that doesn't fit the typical definitions of female or male. Sometimes a female or male **gender** is assigned to an **intersex** person at birth through surgery, if external **genitals** are not obviously male or female. **Intersex** babies are always assigned a legal **gender**, but sometimes when they grow up, they don't identify with the **gender** selected for them.

Intimacy: The closeness you feel when you share your private and personal self with someone else.

Intimate partner violence (IPV): A pattern of emotional, verbal, physical, or **sexual abuse** in the context of an intimate relationship. Also called "domestic violence," "partner abuse," "relationship abuse," and "dating violence."

Intrauterine device (IUD): A tiny device that's placed in the **uterus** to prevent **pregnancy**. It's safe, long-term, reversible, and one of the most effective **birth control** methods available. One **IUD**, the ParaGard, uses copper to prevent **pregnancy**. Others use **hormones** to prevent **pregnancy**.

J:

Jealousy: Feelings of anxiety about a partner or crush's attention, **love**, or commitment. Fear that a partner has feelings for someone else.

Jock itch: A very common fungal skin infection on the **scrotum**, **penis**, or groin area. Caused by wearing tight clothing, sweating a lot, or not drying the **genitals** carefully after bathing. **Jock itch** can cause a reddish, scaly rash that can become inflamed, itchy, and painful.

K:

Kegel exercises: The tightening and releasing of the muscles that stop urination in order to prevent and improve urinary incontinence, improve sexual sensation, and aid recovery of **vaginal** muscle tone after childbirth. Because they exercise internal muscles, **kegels** can be done anywhere, anytime.

L:

Labia: The lips of the **vulva**.

Labia majora: The outer lips of the **vulva**.

Labia minora: The inner lips of the **vulva**.

Labor: The process of childbirth, including everything from the **contractions** of the **uterus** and dilation of the **cervix** to delivery of the infant and finally the **placenta**.

Lesbian: A woman who's sexually or romantically attracted to other women.

LGBTQ+: Stands for **lesbian**, **gay**, **bisexual**, **transgender**, and **questioning** (or, alternatively, "**queer**").

Libido: Feeling of sexual desire.

Love: A strong caring for someone else. It comes in many forms. There can be **love** for romantic partners and also for close friends, for parents and children, for pets, for nature, or for something religious/spiritual.

Lube/lubricant: A water-based, silicone-based, or oil-based product used to increase slipperiness and reduce friction during **sex**.

Lust: Sexual desire for someone.

M:

Mammogram: Breast cancer screening that takes X-rays of the **breasts** to detect cancer before they can be felt.

Marriage: The socially and legally recognized union of a couple as spouses.

Masculine: Characteristics and ways of appearing and behaving that society associates with being a boy or a man.

Mastectomy: The surgical removal of a breast.

Masturbation: Touching one's own body/**genitals** for sexual pleasure.

Medication abortion / medical abortion: The use of a combination of drugs to end a **pregnancy**. Also called the "abortion pill."

Menopause: When menstruation stops because of hormonal changes. Usually happens between the ages of 45 and 55, but sometimes **menopause** happens earlier due to certain medical conditions.

Menstrual cup: A latex or silicone receptacle that fits in the **vagina** to collect **menstrual flow**.

Menstrual cycle: The time from the first day of one **period** to the first day of the next **period**. During the **menstrual cycle**, the lining of the **uterus** grows, an **egg** is released by the **ovaries**, and the uterine lining sheds.

Menstrual flow: Blood and discharge that are passed out of the **uterus** through the **vagina** during the beginning of the **menstrual cycle**.

Method effectiveness: How well a particular type of **birth control** prevents **pregnancy**.

Miscarriage: When an **embryo** or **fetus** dies before the 20th week of **pregnancy**.

Misogyny: Dislike, contempt for, or hatred of women.

Monogamy: When two people decide to have **sex** only with each other and no one else.

Morning sickness: Nausea and vomiting that happens during the **first trimester** of **pregnancy**.

Morning wood: Slang for having an erect **penis** when waking up. People who have **penises** can have several **erections** at night as part of their sleep cycle. Very often, when they wake up, they're still erect. Also called "nocturnal penile tumescence."

Morning-after pill: **Emergency contraception** that can be used within 120 hours (five days) of unprotected **vaginal sex** to decrease the chance of **pregnancy**.

Multiple orgasms: The occurrence of more than one **orgasm** within one sexual experience.

Mutual masturbation: When people masturbate in each other's presence.

N:

Nipple: The dark tissue in the center of the areola of each breast in someone of any **gender**. **Nipples** can stand erect when stimulated by touch or cold. The **nipples** can also release milk in people who are breastfeeding.

Nocturnal emission: Commonly known as a "**wet dream**"; **ejaculation** while sleeping, which most often occurs during **puberty**.

Nocturnal orgasm: A sexual **climax** during sleep.

Nurse practitioner: A registered nurse who has been trained to provide primary health care, including many services also performed by doctors.

NuvaRing: The brand name of the hormonal **birth control** ring available in the U.S. The **NuvaRing** is placed inside the **vagina**, and needs to be replaced each month.

O:

Oral contraceptive: Another name for the **birth control pill**.

Oral herpes: An infection of the mouth with **herpes** simplex virus 1 or **herpes** simplex virus 2. Symptoms are commonly known as cold sores.

Oral sex: **Sex** involving the mouth and **genitals**, including cunnilingus, anilingus, and fellatio.

Orgasm: The peak of **sexual arousal**, when all the muscles that were tightened during **sexual arousal** relax, usually causing a very pleasurable feeling.

Out: Short for "**out** of the **closet**." Being open about your **sexual orientation** or **gender identity**.

Outercourse: Sexual activity that doesn't include **vaginal** or **anal sex**.

Outing: Revealing someone else's **sexual orientation** or **gender identity** that they may not have shared or wanted to be shared.

Ovaries: The two organs that store and release **eggs**. **Ovaries** also produce **hormones**, including **estrogen**, **progesterone**, and **testosterone**.

Over-the-counter: Available without a prescription from a nurse or doctor.

Ovulation: When an **ovary** releases an **egg**.

P:

Pansexual: Having sexual or **romantic attraction** to people of all **genders**.

Pap smear: A term commonly used to describe a **Pap test**, which looks for abnormal, precancerous, or cancerous growths on the **cervix**.

Pap test: A test to look for abnormal, precancerous, or cancerous growths on the **cervix**. Sometimes called a **Pap smear**.

Parental consent: A requirement that one or both parents give permission for a minor (someone under the age of 18) to do something. Many states have mandatory **parental consent** laws regarding **abortion** services for minors. Most states don't require **parental consent** for services like **birth control** or **STI** testing.

Pelvic exam: A physical exam of the **vulva**, **vagina**, **cervix**, **uterus**, and **ovaries**. May include a Pap or **HPV** test, but not always.

Pelvic inflammatory disease (PID): An infection in the **uterus**, **fallopian tubes**, and/or **ovaries** that can lead to **infertility**, **ectopic pregnancy**, and chronic pain. It's often caused by untreated **STIs** like **gonorrhea** and **chlamydia**.

Penis: A reproductive and **sex** organ that's made of spongy tissue. The spongy tissue fills with blood during sexual **excitement**, a process known as **erection** (getting hard). Urine and **semen** pass through the **penis**.

PEP (post-exposure prophylaxis): Medicine that helps prevent **HIV** (or other infections) if started within a few days after being exposed.

Perfect use: How effective a **birth control** method would be if always used exactly the right way. See "**typical use**."

Period: Menstruation. The monthly flow of blood and tissue from the **uterus** and out the **vagina**.

Pill, the: Short for the **birth control** pill.

Placenta: The organ formed on the wall of the **uterus** that provides oxygen and other nourishment to a **fetus** during **pregnancy**, and through which waste products are eliminated from a **fetus**.

Plan B: A brand of **emergency contraception** pill made from levonorgestrel, the same kind of **hormone** found in **birth control** pills. Available **over the counter** to anyone of any age or **gender** in the US.

Platonic: Not sexual.

Polyamory: Having sexual or romantic relationships with more than one person at a time with the consent of all people involved.

Pornography (porn): Video, photos or words that are made for sexual **excitement**.

Postpartum: Following childbirth.

Precum: Slang for pre-ejaculate, the liquid that oozes out of the **penis** during sexual **excitement** before **ejaculation**. Sometimes, for some people, it has a small amount of **sperm** in it.

Pregnancy: When someone is carrying a developing **fetus** in their **uterus**. It begins with the **implantation** of the **pre-embryo** and progresses through the embryonic and fetal stages until birth, unless it's ended by **miscarriage** or **abortion**. It lasts about 40 weeks from **implantation** to birth.

PrEP (pre-exposure prophylaxis): A medicine taken daily to reduce the risk of getting **HIV**.

Pro-choice: Supporting the right to a safe, legal **abortion**.

Progesterone: A hormone produced in the ovaries that helps regulate puberty, menstruation, and pregnancy.

Prostate: A gland that produces a fluid which helps **sperm** move. The **prostate** can be very sensitive to the touch, and many people enjoy stimulating the **prostate** for sexual pleasure.

Puberty: The time between childhood and adulthood when people mature physically and sexually. **Puberty** is marked by changes such as breast development and menstruation or hair growth and **ejaculation**.

Pubic hair: Hair that grows around the **sex** organs. **Pubic hair** is a **secondary sex characteristic** that appears during **puberty**.

Pubic lice: Tiny insects that can be sexually transmitted. They live in **pubic hair** and cause intense itching in the **genitals**.

Pulling out / pull-out method: Pulling the **penis** out of the **vagina** before **ejaculation** in order to avoid **pregnancy**. Also called "**withdrawal**."

Q:

Queef: The sound made when air is released from the **vagina**. Air is often pushed into the **vagina** during **vaginal sex** or penetration with **tampons**, fingers, or **sex** toys.

Queer: A word that can refer to a variety of sexual identities and **gender identities** that are anything other than **straight** and **cisgender**. In the past **queer** was used as a slur, and may still be offensive to some. However, many people use the word with pride to identify themselves.

Questioning: Being unsure about your **sexual orientation** or **gender identity**.

R:

Rape: **Sexual intercourse** without consent.

Reproductive cell: Unique cells—**egg** and **sperm**—that can join to make reproduction possible.

Reproductive organs: The **fallopian tubes**, **ovaries**, **uterus**, **vagina**, **penis**, and **testes**. Organs that relate to reproduction.

Romantic attraction: A desire for an intimate (but not necessarily sexual) connection with another person.

S:

Safer sex: Ways in which people reduce the risk of getting **sexually transmitted infections**, including **HIV**. A more precise term than "safe **sex**," because no **sex** act is completely safe from the possibility of passing a **sexually transmitted infection**.

Sanitary pad: An absorbent reusable or disposable lining made of cotton or similar fibers that's worn against the **vulva** to absorb **menstrual flow**.

Scrotum: A sac of skin, divided into two parts, that holds the **testicles**.

Second trimester: The second three months of **pregnancy**.

Secondary sex characteristics: Features of the body that are caused by **hormones**. They develop during **puberty**, or can be brought on by **hormone** replacement therapy (HRT). For people with **vaginas**, these include breast development and widened hips. For people with **penises**, they include facial hair development and voice deepening. And everyone develops **pubic hair** and underarm hair.

Self-esteem: Feeling worthwhile.

Semen: Fluid containing **sperm** that's ejaculated from the **penis** during **orgasm**. **Semen** is composed of fluid from the seminal vesicles, fluid from the **prostate**, and **sperm** from the **testes**.

Seminal fluid: A liquid that nourishes and helps **sperm** to move. Made in the seminal vesicles.

Seminal vesicle: One of two small organs located beneath the **bladder** and connected to the **urethra** that produce **seminal fluid**.

Sex: A label assigned at birth of female, male, or sometimes **intersex**. Also, the act of **vaginal**, anal, or manual (using hands) **intercourse**, or oral-**genital** stimulation, with a partner.

Sex assignment: The designation of biological **sex**—female, male, or **intersex**—usually made by a doctor at the birth of a child. The **sex** that appears on a person's birth certificate.

Sex cell: A **reproductive cell**—**egg** or **sperm**.

Sexism: Systemic and individual discrimination against women.

Sexting: Sending sexual text messages or images.

Sexual abuse: Sexual activity that's harmful, exploitative, or not consensual.

Sexual arousal: **Erotic excitement**.

Sexual assault: The use of force or **coercion**, physical or psychological, to make a person engage in sexual activity.

Sexual harassment: Unwanted sexual advances from someone. Includes suggestive gestures, language, or touching.

Sexual health: Enjoying emotional, physical, and social well-being in regard to one's **sexuality**, including free and responsible sexual expression that enriches one's life. (**Sexual health** is not only the absence of sexual dysfunction or disease.)

Sexual identity: Your understanding of your own **sex**, **gender identity**, **sexual orientation**, and sexual expression/preferences.

Sexual intercourse: Usually, **sex** that includes penetration of the **vagina** with a **penis**. Can also describe penetration of the anus with a **penis**.

Sexual orientation: Identities that describe what **gender(s)** a person is romantically and/or sexually attracted to. There are many **sexual orientations.** Some common **sexual orientations** include **gay**, **lesbian**, **straight**, and **bisexual**.

Sexual preference: People, activities, or other things that you like sexually.

Sexuality: Sex, **gender identity**, **sexual orientation**, **sexual preference**, and the way these things interact with emotional, physical, social, and spiritual life. **Sexuality** is shaped by your family and the social norms of your community.

Sexually transmitted disease (STD): Infections that are passed from one person to another during **vaginal**, anal, or **oral sex**, or sexual skin-to-skin contact. More accurately called **sexually transmitted infection**.

Sexually transmitted infection (STI): Infections that are passed from one person to another during **vaginal**, **anal**, or **oral sex**, or sexual skin-to-skin contact. Commonly known as **sexually transmitted disease**.

Shaft: A structure of **erectile tissue** and nerves that's shaped like a column and forms the body of the **penis** and **clitoris**.

Speculum: A plastic or metal instrument used to separate the walls of the **vagina** so a doctor or nurse can examine the **vagina** and **cervix**.

Sperm: A **reproductive cell** that combines with an **egg** to cause a **pregnancy**. Made in the **testes**.

Spotting: Light bleeding that happens not during a menstrual **period**.

Squirting: **Ejaculation** from people with **vulvas**, sometimes called "female **ejaculation**." The fluid comes from the Skene's glands, which are located in the **vulva** near the opening of the **urethra**. **Squirting** happens in about one out of 10 women.

Stalking: Following or tracking someone in person or online without their consent.

Statutory rape: Legally, sexual contact between an adult and anyone who is below the **age of consent**, whether or not the contact is voluntary.

Stereotype: A widely accepted judgment or bias regarding a person or group.

Sterilization: Surgical methods of **birth control** that are intended to be permanent—blocking of the **fallopian tubes** for women or the **vas deferens** for men.

Stigma: Severe disapproval/judgment for a behavior that's reinforced by society/culture.

Straight: Being attracted to people of the other **gender**. **Heterosexual**.

Syphilis: A bacterial **sexually transmitted infection** that is easily cured with **antibiotics**, but can cause permanent damage if left untreated.

T:

Tampon: A firm, disposable roll of absorbent cotton or other fiber that goes inside the **vagina** to absorb menstrual blood.

Testes: Two ball-like glands inside the **scrotum** that produce **hormones**, including **testosterone**. Each testis also encloses several hundred small lobes, which contain the tiny, threadlike seminiferous tubules that produce **sperm**. Also called "**testicles**."

Testicles: Two ball-like glands inside the **scrotum** that produce **hormones**, including **testosterone**. Each **testicle** also encloses several hundred small lobes, which contain the tiny, threadlike seminiferous tubules that produce **sperm**. Also called "**testes**."

Testosterone: An androgen **hormone** produced in the **testes** and in smaller amounts in the **ovaries**. Generally associated with **masculine secondary sex characteristics**. Can be taken synthetically as **gender affirming** treatment for **trans** men.

Third trimester: The last three months of **pregnancy**.

Toxic shock syndrome: A rare but very dangerous overgrowth of bacteria in the **vagina**. Symptoms include vomiting, high fever, diarrhea, and a sunburn-type rash. A possible result of leaving an object (including **tampons** and **birth control** sponges) in the **vagina** for too long.

Trans: Short for **transgender**. A general term used to describe someone whose **gender** expression/**gender identity** are different than the **sex** they were assigned at birth. Some people put an asterisk on the end of **trans*** to expand the word to include all people with non-conforming **gender** identities and expressions.

Transgender: A general term used to describe someone whose **gender** expression/**gender identity** are different than the **sex** they were assigned at birth.

Transition: The process of a person changing to present as the **gender** they identify as. **Transitioning** means different things to different people. It may involve any of the following: **coming out** to one's family, changing the pronouns and words used to describe one's **gender**, dressing differently, changing one's name, or beginning **gender** affirming health care.

Transphobia: Fear and hatred of people who are, or are perceived to be, **trans**-identified or **gender non-conforming**.

Tubal ligation: Surgical blocking of the **fallopian tubes** by tying them off. A form of **sterilization**—permanent **birth control**.

Two-spirit: An umbrella term for **gender identities** common in American Indian/First Nations/Native American cultures. Refers to people who have both **masculine** and **feminine** parts of their identity, and are treated as a third **gender** within those cultures.

Typical use: The effectiveness of a particular **birth control** method in the population, taking into account when people don't always use their method consistently or correctly. Since this looks at real world use, it's a more accurate way to describe how many people get pregnant using a method.

U:

Ultrasound: A medical test that creates an image of internal organs by bouncing sound waves off the internal organs. Frequently used to find or monitor a **pregnancy**, but has a variety of medical uses.

Urethra: A tube that empties the **bladder** and carries urine to the **urethral** opening (the hole you pee out of). The **urethra** also carries ejaculate and pre-ejaculate in people with **penises**.

Urinary tract infection (UTI): A bacterial infection of the **bladder**, the ureters, or the **urethra**. It is not sexually transmitted. The most common symptom is a frequent urge to pee and pain while peeing. Curable with **antibiotics**.

Uterus: The pear-shaped, reproductive organ from which people menstruate and where a **pregnancy** develops. Also called "womb."

V:

Vagina: The stretchy passage that connects the **vulva** with the **cervix** and **uterus**. It's where menstrual comes out of the body, a baby comes out of the body through childbirth, and/or one place sexual penetration (by a **penis**, finger, sex toy, etc.) can happen. During menstruation, it's where **tampons** or **menstrual cups** are placed.

Vaginal sex: **Sex** in which a **penis** enters a **vagina**. Also called "**vaginal intercourse**" or "**penis**-in-**vagina sex**."

Vas deferens: A long, narrow tube that carries **sperm** from each **epididymis** to the seminal vesicles during **ejaculation**. This is the tube that's cut for a **vasectomy**, stopping **sperm** from leaving the body.

Vasectomy: Surgical blocking of the vasa deferentia (each **vas deferens**) for permanent **birth control**.

Vibrator: An electrically powered **sex** toy that applies vibrations to parts of the body for **sexual pleasure**.

Virginity: Having never had **sex**. May mean different things to different people. For example, many people think you "lose your **virginity**" when you have **vaginal sex**. Others think that you lose your **virginity** if you have other kinds of sexual activity, like **oral sex** or **anal sex**.

Vulva: The external **sex** organs that include the **clitoris, labia (majora and minora)**, opening to the **vagina** (introitus), opening to the **urethra**, and two Bartholin's glands.

W:

Wet dreams: **Erotic** dreams that can lead to **ejaculation** or

vaginal lubrication. Common during **puberty**. See "**nocturnal emission**."

Withdrawal: Pulling the **penis** out of the **vagina** before **ejaculation** in order to avoid **pregnancy**. Also called "**pulling out**" or the "**pull-out method**."

X:

Xe (xe, xem, xyr, xyrs, xemself): A **gender-neutral** pronoun (or set of pronouns) some people use for themselves to replace "he," "she," or "they."

Y:

Yeast infection: A type of vaginitis caused by an overgrowth of a yeast that naturally lives in the **vagina**/on the body, called candida albicans. **Yeast infections** may also occur in the **penis** or mouth. A **yeast infection** in the mouth or throat is called "thrush."

Z:

Ze (ze, zir, zirs, zirself): A **gender-neutral** pronoun (or set of pronouns) some people use for themselves to replace "he," "she," or "they."

Zygote: The single-celled organism that results from the joining of the **egg** and **sperm** (**fertilization**).

ACKNOWLEDGMENTS

First, it is important to thank all the sex educators out there. All of them. Some of you are in schools, some of you work for non-profits, some of you do it just because young people trust you and know you are a safe adult to talk to. To all of you, thank you. This book is dedicated to your service and passion and we, the educators at the Responsible Sex Education Institute of Planned Parenthood of the Rocky Mountains, are proud to stand with you in this work.

A special thank-you to all of the young people who have texted us your questions. We are committed to being a resource for you, regardless of where you live. Thank you for trusting us.

Thank you to Planned Parenthood Federation of America and Trans Student Education Resources. It is an honor to work in this space with you, and we greatly appreciate your support as we work to arm young people with the information they need to live healthy lives.

We want to thank Planned Parenthoods everywhere, especially Planned Parenthood of the Rocky Mountains. We will continue to fight for the reproductive freedom that *all* people deserve, and we are proud to be a part of this work.

Finally, we want to thank the incredible staff at the Responsible Sex Education Institute. Specifically, we would like to thank: Molly Alderton, Daniela Fellman, Meghan Hilton, Julie LaBarr, Alison Macklin, Elizabeth Weyer-Hudson, Becki Jones, Liza Bley, Rebekkah Abeyta, Tati Santos, Lizzie Smalls, Ryan Garcia, Brandi Lucero, Jax Sugars, Myra Llerenas, Andy

Nuanhngam, Persephone Wilson, Brenda Hernandez, Julissa Salas, Dawn Canty, Rosita Castillo, and Robert Thurmond.

We are greatly appreciative of your contributions to the book and the ICYC text line.

END NOTES

1 Parenthood, Planned. "State of Sex Education in USA | Health Education in Schools." Planned Parenthood. Accessed February 01, 2019. https://www.plannedparenthood.org/learn/for-educators/whats-state-sex-education-us.

2 "Sex and HIV Education." Guttmacher Institute. January 02, 2019. Accessed February 01, 2019. https://www.guttmacher.org/state-policy/explore/sex-and-hiv-education.

3 "Sex and HIV Education." Guttmacher Institute. January 02, 2019. Accessed February 01, 2019. https://www.guttmacher.org/state-policy/explore/sex-and-hiv-education.

4 Jio, Sarah. "All the Ways You Can Burn Calories During Sex." Woman's Day. January 06, 2019. Accessed February 01, 2019. https://www.womansday.com/relationships/sex-tips/advice/a1922/8-sexy-ways-to-burn-calories-110923/.

5 MacGill, Markus. "What Is the Average Penis Size?" Medical News Today. July 09, 2018. Accessed February 01, 2019. https://www.medicalnewstoday.com/articles/271647.php.

6 "How Many Eggs Does a Woman Have?" WebMD. Accessed February 01, 2019. https://www.webmd.com/menopause/qa/how-many-eggs-does-a-woman-have.

7 "How a Man Produces 1,500 Sperm a Second." National Geographic. March 19, 2010. Accessed February 01, 2019. https://news.nationalgeographic.com/news/2010/03/100318-men-sperm-1500-stem-cells-second-male-birth-control/.

8 Pappas, Stephanie. "Bears Not Attracted to Menstruating Women." LiveScience. August 25, 2012. Accessed February 01, 2019. https://www.livescience.com/22688-myth-bears-attack-menstruating-women.html.)

9 "Science & Nature - Human Body and Mind - Teenagers." BBC. Accessed February 01, 2019. http://www.bbc.co.uk/science/humanbody/body/articles/lifecycle/teenagers/breast_development.shtml.

10 Stöppler, Melissa Conrad. "Symptoms of Menopause: At What Age Does It Start?" EMedicineHealth - Health and Medical Information Produced by Doctors. Accessed February 01, 2019. https://www.emedicinehealth.com/menopause/article_em.htm.

11 Maguire, Katie, and Katie Maguire. "Does Sleeping in a Bra Lead to Breast Cancer?" Well+Good. October 17, 2018. Accessed February 01, 2019. https://www.wellandgood.com/good-advice/sleeping-in-bra-breast-cancer-connection/slide/2/.

12 Teen Rights to Sex Ed, Birth Control and More in New Mexico - Sex, Etc. Accessed February 01, 2019. https://sexetc.org/about/.

13 Parenthood, Planned. "Is My Menstrual Cycle Normal? | Facts & Information." Planned Parenthood. Accessed February 01, 2019. https://www.plannedparenthood.org/learn/health-and-wellness/menstruation/how-do-i-know-if-my-menstrual-cycle-normal.

14 "Why Do You Get Morning Wood? Believe It Or Not, There's an Important Scientific Reason." Men's Health. July 23, 2018. Accessed February 01, 2019. https://www.menshealth.com/sex-women/a19548523/what-is-morning-wood/.

15 Care.com, Inc. "When Do Girls Stop Growing?" Care.com. Accessed February 01, 2019. https://www.care.com/c/stories/4218/when-do-girls-stop-growing/.

16 "What's an Adam's Apple? (for Kids)." KidsHealth. June 2016. Accessed February 01, 2019. https://kidshealth.org/en/kids/adams-apple.html.

17 "The Gender Unicorn." Trans Student Educational Resources. Accessed February 01, 2019. http://www.transstudent.org/gender/.

18 Parenthood, Planned. "LGBTQ Info For Teens | Sexual Orientation & Gender Identity." Planned Parenthood. Accessed February 01, 2019. https://www.plannedparenthood.org/learn/teens/lgbtq/sexual-orientation.

19 Parenthood, Planned. "Teens Coming Out | How to Come Out to Your Parents & Family." Planned Parenthood. Accessed February 01, 2019. https://www.plannedparenthood.org/learn/teens/lgbtq/coming-out.

20 "STD Facts - Human Papillomavirus (HPV)." Centers for Disease Control and Prevention. Accessed February 01, 2019. https://www.cdc.gov/std/hpv/stdfact-hpv.htm.

21 Escobar, Samantha. "The Condom Timeline: A Detailed History Of

Wrapping It Up." YourTango. August 06, 2013. Accessed February 01, 2019. https://www.yourtango.com/2013189729/condom-timeline-detailed-history-wrapping-it.

22 "Detailed STD Facts - Chlamydia." Centers for Disease Control and Prevention. Accessed February 01, 2019. https://www.cdc.gov/std/chlamydia/stdfact-chlamydia-detailed.htm.

23 Boskey, Elizabeth, and Susan Olender. "Waiting for the Right Time to Get Tested If You Have an STD." Verywell Health. Accessed February 01, 2019. https://www.verywellhealth.com/how-long-should-i-wait-for-std-testing-3132737.

24 "Early Pregnancy Symptoms." HealthLine. September 5, 2018. Accessed February 1, 2019. https://www.healthline.com/health/pregnancy/early-symptoms-timeline.

25 "How Common Are Miscarriages?" WebMD. Accessed February 01, 2019. http://www.webmd.com/baby/qa/how-common-are-miscarriages.

26 "Patterned Breathing During Labor: Techniques and Benefits." American Pregnancy Association. September 26, 2017. Accessed February 01, 2019. http://americanpregnancy.org/labor-and-birth/patterned-breathing/.

27 "Sex after Pregnancy: Set Your Own Timeline." Mayo Clinic. July 07, 2018. Accessed February 01, 2019. https://www.mayoclinic.org/healthy-lifestyle/labor-and-delivery/in-depth/sex-after-pregnancy/art-20045669.

28 "Is It Possible to Get Pregnant from Swimming in a Pool? How Fast Is Sperm Killed by Chlorine and Other Chemicals?" U by Kotex®. Accessed February 01, 2019. https://www.ubykotex.com/en-us/periods/vaginal-and-reproductive-health/is-it-possible-to-get-pregnant-from-swimming-in-a-pool-how.

29 CBS News. "Sperm: 15 Crazy Things You Should Know." CBS News. September 19, 2011. Accessed February 01, 2019. https://www.cbsnews.com/pictures/sperm-15-crazy-things-you-should-know/7/.

30 Callahan, Alice. "What Causes Morning Sickness?" The New York Times. August 03, 2018. Accessed February 01, 2019. https://www.nytimes.com/2018/08/03/well/what-causes-morning-sickness.html.

31 "Promoting Pregnancy Wellness." American Pregnancy Association. Accessed February 01, 2019. http://americanpregnancy.org/.

32 Raine-Bennett, Tina. "Does Using Birth Control Hurt My Chances of Getting Pregnant Later?" Bedsider. Accessed February 01, 2019. https://www.bedsider.org/features/76-birth-control-and-infertility-does-using-birth-control-hurt-my-chances-of-getting-pregnant-later.

33 Gallo MF, Lopez LM, Grimes DA, Carayon F, Schulz KF, Helmerhorst FM. "Combination contraceptives: effects on weight." Cochrane Database of Systematic Reviews 2014, Issue 1. Art. No.: CD003987. https://www.cochrane.org/CD003987/FERTILREG_effect-of-birth-control-pills-and-patches-on-weight.

34 Parenthood, Planned. "What Kind of Emergency Contraception Is Best For Me?" Planned Parenthood. Accessed February 01, 2019. https://www.plannedparenthood.org/learn/morning-after-pill-emergency-contraception/which-kind-emergency-contraception-should-i-use.

35 "Fertility Awareness: Natural Family Planning (NFP)." American Pregnancy Association. September 02, 2016. Accessed February 01, 2019. http://americanpregnancy.org/preventing-pregnancy/natural-family-planning/.

36 Ppfaq. "Plannedparenthood." Planned Parenthood. August 05, 2016. Accessed February 01, 2019. http://plannedparenthood.tumblr.com/post/148506806862/understanding-consent-is-as-easy-as-fries-consent.

37 "Bystander Intervention Tips." It's On Us. Accessed February 1, 2019. https://www.itsonus.org/wp-content/uploads/2017/04/IOU-Bystander-Intervention-Tips.pdf.

NOTES

....

....

....

....

....

....

....

....

....

....

....

....

....

....

....

....

....

....

....

....

....

....

....

....

....

....

....

....

....

....

....

....

....

....

....

....

....

....

....

....

....

....

....